Presents

D0506641

Uncluttering
Your Space

Presents

Uncluttering Your Space

The Learning Annex
with Ann Sullivan

WILEY

Wiley Publishing, Inc.

For general information on our other products and services or to obtain technical support please contact our Customer Care Department within the U.S. at 800-762-2974, outside the U.S. at 317-572-3993 or fax 317-572-4002.

Wiley also publishes its books in a variety of electronic formats. Some content that appears in print may not be available in electronic books.

ISBN: 0-7645-4145-5

Cataloging-in-Publication Data available from the Library of Congress.

Manufactured in the United States of America

10 9 8 7 6 5 4 3 2 1

PRAISE FOR THE LEARNING ANNEX

"Because I'm so busy I really don't have time to take a full semester course on anything. The Learning Annex gives me the nuts-and-bolts information I need in just one night. It's great!"

— Rick S.

"This was my first Learning Annex class and I plan on taking many, many more. I can't believe how much I learned from one seminar!"

— Wendy R.

"What I really love about The Learning Annex is the easy-to-understand, practical nature of the classes. It's information you can use immediately."

— Susan L.

"It's one thing to listen to a teacher on a certain subject...but it's much better to hear from a practicing expert in the field. That's what makes the Learning Annex so special."

— Dave L.

"The Learning Annex offers classes that you simply can't find anywhere else. The range of subjects they offer is enormous."

— Sandra S.

"There's no end to the Learning Annex subjects that interest me. Every single class I've taken has taught me all sorts of new things."

— George J.

"Being in a class with other people with the same interests makes learning a lot easier and a lot more fun."

— Yolanda F.

"I met my fiance at a Learning Annex class. I don't remember what I paid, but it was worth it!"

— Kenneth J.

ABOUT ANN SULLIVAN

Ann Sullivan, founder of Ann Sullivan, Inc., provides innovative organizational services to corporations, small businesses, and individuals nationwide. Ms. Sullivan brings to organizing 14 years of experience in the field of legal services where she learned the necessity of maintaining client confidentiality and developed skills that include analytical thinking, problem solving, and attention to detail.

Ann Sullivan, Inc. provides evaluation, organization, and coaching services. This empowers clients with the systems, resources, tools, and training that build order and lead to freedom and peace of mind. Ms. Sullivan's unique philosophy of Organizing People For Life™, combined with her comprehensive approach to organization, has enabled clients to truly transform the way they live and work.

Ann Sullivan relocated to Manhattan from the midwest nine years ago, downsizing from a three-bedroom home to a typical New York City apartment. That move taught her firsthand the benefits of streamlining and organizing one's life. She now owns 60 percent less "stuff" than before and is guided by the advice of artist William Morris: "Have nothing in your home that you do not know to be useful or believe to be beautiful."

Inspired by the possibilities of helping people transform their lives, Ms. Sullivan created her own residential organizing company in 1997. The business quickly expanded to include executives and small businesses and now serves a full range of business and residential clients.

Using her degree in sociology and psychology to build her understanding of how people think and behave, as well as her understanding of the principles of organizing, Ms. Sullivan works to create customized systems to complement her clients' individual styles. By furnishing them with information, products, and services, she brings order and manageability to their daily lives.

Ms. Sullivan is a member of the board of directors of the National Association of Professional Organizers (New York chapter) and serves as chair on the chapter's community service committee. In addition, she is a member of the National Association of Women Business Owners.

Ms. Sullivan's proven methods for successful organizing have been featured on both network and cable television: *The Montel Williams Show, Sheila Bridges Designer Living, Your Morning,* and in a series of interstitials that run on the Fine Living Cable channel. She has also been featured in print: *Modern Bride, The Chicago Tribune, Bottom Line Personal,* and *Dance Retailer News.*

welcome to the Learning Annex

The Learning Annex is North America's largest provider of adult education, dedicated to enhancing the quality of people's lives through informative and inspirational seminars. We offer short, inexpensive courses that provide nuts-and-bolts information on a variety of topics, taught by respected leaders and luminaries in each field. The Learning Annex operates schools in numerous major cities across the United States and Canada, and through its monthly publication, it has emerged as a cultural barometer of what is of interest to the American people.

acknowledgments

The author wishes to thank the Writers' Lifeline, Inc.: Ken Atchity, Andrea McKeown, and especially Julie Mooney. Also thanks to Roxane Cerda and Cindy Kitchel of John Wiley & Sons, and Tim Ryan of Ryan Publishing Group.

table of contents

introduction

People often call me out of desperation. "I feel like my life is unraveling," one of my students lamented. "I can't seem to get a single bill paid on time." Another student admitted, "My house is such a mess, I can't even invite friends over." "There are never enough hours in the day," a working mom told me. "I spend forever answering phone calls and dealing with paperwork, and I never find time for the most important stuff, like hanging out with my kids."

It's practically an epidemic in our culture today: We have more money, more possessions, more means of communication, and more conveniences than ever before—far more than our parents or grandparents could ever have dreamed of—yet so many of us feel as though our lives are careening out of control. Our time doesn't belong to us anymore, and our possessions have somehow begun to possess *us*.

How did our lives get so crazy?

With the widespread use of cell phones, e-mails, pagers, and faxes, we've made ourselves far more accessible. People now expect us to be available immediately, anytime, anywhere. It's no longer acceptable to get back to someone within 24 hours. Now, everyone expects a response within a few hours, if not minutes.

Technology in the home and workplace was supposed to make our lives easier, simpler. In many instances, however, it's done the opposite. Marketers and advertisers have convinced us that the right gadget will make life more manageable; in fact, many of these devices simply add clutter to our homes, offices, minds, and lives.

We're bombarded. We've allowed others to take control of our time and our lifestyle. No wonder we're overwhelmed.

It can be even worse when home and work collide. Take a peek in the average home office, and you'll find a mountain of paperwork waiting to be filed. The average disorganized person has more than 3,000 documents at home. Statistics show that we'll actually reference only 20 percent of those documents, yet those documents are constantly affecting their owner's concentration, taking up space, and creating a frustrating sense of unfinished work. The stacks of paper just keep growing—who has the time to file all that stuff? Before we know it, the mountain overflows from a tray into a box and then from a box to several haphazard stacks on the floor.

Stuff it all in a closet, you say? Well, that's a problem. Open any closet in the average home, and you'd better be prepared to jump back. There's a monster in there. There's no telling what forgotten treasures that closet might contain: the good stuff is buried under mounds of unwanted gifts, broken household objects, and impulse bargain buys that just weren't quite what you wanted.

Our homes are so stuffed with possessions that we hardly know what we own. Most of our things are not even bringing us pleasure or serving a purpose, yet we continue to store them, move them, insure them, clean them, keep them safe, and take responsibility for them. They've taken on a life of their own, and now they're taking over ours!

Advertisers have trumpeted a "more is better" philosophy, and we consumers have bought it lock, stock, and barrel. Marketers successfully create a sense of urgency: if you see something you like, you'd better buy it *now*! Advertising bombards us wherever we go—billboards, TVs, doctors' offices, the Internet—they're even making wider gas nozzles at the pumps to make room for a little advertising plaque. It's not enough that grocery stores hang garish banners on every available space; they're now sticking product ads all over the floors. They even advertise to us in public bathrooms.

Many of us complain about a bloat of possessions, yet we keep buying more and bringing it home. Talk to anyone who's recently moved. Chances are they'll tell you, "I'm opening up all these boxes and wondering why I thought this stuff was important enough to haul 2,000 miles?"

How did we let this happen? I think it's because we've bought the myth. We have come to believe that we can have it all and do it all. But what's the point of trying to have it all if we can't even enjoy what we've got?

The truth is, we can't have it all, but we *can* have what's *important*. The key is to know what that is and create a plan for achieving it. Life shouldn't be lived by default.

When you renovate your home, you don't just grab a sledgehammer and start whacking at a wall. You begin with an end in mind, and you take the necessary steps to achieve it. If we want specific conditions in our lives, we have to arrange our lives to create those conditions. It is possible to organize your physical environment to reflect a sense of purpose and meaning. Instead of living in a state of chaos, you can create a calm, orderly environment that's as functional as it is aesthetically pleasing.

This book will show you how to take your life back from the objects and devices that have claimed it. I've included in these 15 lessons the principles and exercises I've used with my clients through my company, Ann Sullivan—Organizing People For Life™, and have taught to students in my Learning Annex Seminars.

When someone calls me for help, the first thing I ask is, "What triggered your call? Why are you calling at this particular time in your life?" Typically, these people have found themselves at a state of transition: They're having a baby, getting a divorce, downsizing, upsizing, or crossing some other threshold. They're stepping back, often for the first time in years, to take a look at the bigger picture of their lives, and they're aghast at what they see. Many have a gut-level understanding that their clutter is holding them back in some fashion.

"I just missed my third doctor appointment in a row!"

"I still have all my notebooks from high school—like I'm ever going to need those again!"

"My cabinets are stuffed! Just yesterday, I opened a kitchen cabinet and a whole stack of things fell right on my baby's head. Thank goodness it was only Tupperware, but. . . ."

Once we identify the juncture they've reached in their lives, I ask them, "What are your goals from here?" Our primary job is to create the environment that supports those goals. We'll list your goals and activities. Then we'll look at every room in your house, from both a "macro" and a "micro" perspective. What activities does this room support? What areas serve which goals? We'll find ways to make the space you have serve the goals you've chosen.

Then we need to inventory what you own. You can't work with what you don't know you have. You've got to find out what's yours, put hands on it, sort it, and determine its function. If it doesn't have one, get rid of it.

a note from
the instructor

YOU'VE GOT MAIL…AND MOST OF IT'S JUNK

According to the U.S. Postal Service, we receive more mail in a week than our parents did in a year and our grandparents in a lifetime. The Consumer Research Institute, an anti-junk mail organization, estimates that we waste a whopping eight months of our lives dealing with this unwanted mail.

I've had many a client respond in horror to this idea. "You mean I have to *throw away* my old (busted tennis racket, ugly vase, photo of an anonymous relative—you fill in the blank), but I love that thing!" I'm not saying get rid of the things you're genuinely attached to. I want you to become aware of what you have, what it's doing in your life, and how it's serving you. You're now going to be owning consciously, instead of owning by default. Because your possessions affect you, whether you're aware of them or not, you owe it to yourself to get rid of the dead weight.

As you streamline and de-junk your life, you'll often be aware that you're venturing into lonely territory. It takes some courage to let go of your stuff in a stuff-crazy world. You won't be living the way the majority is living, and that's OK—don't forget that the majority is *stressed out*.

Isn't it better to lead a good fashion than to follow a bad one?

HOW TO USE THIS BOOK

This book is designed to be a "seminar in print," to allow readers to feel as much as possible as though they're attending one of our evening courses. We've divided the book into topics, titled "Lessons," each of which can be read within 10 to 15 minutes. We have designed this book to be completed in a single sit-down reading. Two types of sidebars will help give you additional, fun, and useful information:

- **A Note from the Instructor:** Insider tips from your instructor, Ann Sullivan.

- **Student Experiences:** Words from seminar students—just like you—who are willing to share their experience in decluttering their lives.

why we're drowning in clutter

Clutter in Today's Society • The Reasons We Hoard Things • Why We Don't Want to Clean Up

The odds are stacked against us. Our modern society is the most clutter-prone society in the world for one simple reason: We've got so much *stuff!* We're an affluent society, so we have the means to produce and purchase a dazzling array of material goods. We've also attached a tremendous amount of cultural and personal meaning to the ownership of objects. Add to this mix an advertising industry that works overtime to condition our psyches to become mindless buying machines, and it's no wonder we're wallowing in excess stuff.

Let's look at some of the ways our culture sets us up for an overload of possessions.

IT'S ALL AROUND US

Never before in human history has there been such a blinding array of material goods that can be had so cheaply and so easily. Never has there been a people so rich in cash and credit as we are—and so eager to exchange their hard-earned wages for personal items.

Even when we're not on a buying frenzy, the stuff still finds its way home with us. Have you noticed that every time you attend a conference you leave with binders, pens, papers, and all kinds of promotional products? I once went to a student's house where she showed me her collection of more than 500 pens, and she hadn't bought a single one of them! That's the insidious thing about freebies: They multiply!

If you think we're behaving poorly as grownups, look at the way we're setting up our kids for even more pointless stuff-consumption. Every time your children go to a birthday party, they come home with a bag of little cheapo toys that you'll be digging out of the sofa cushions for the next several months. Children can't even go to a fast-food restaurant without bringing home another useless plastic toy.

When we let our kids collect more junk than they can possibly deal with, we're being unfair to them. Most adults would find it a challenge to organize what the average kid owns today. How are the kids going to learn order and tidiness when they have such an overwhelming mass of possessions to deal with? When the flow of free, valueless stuff never ends, how will they learn to work for and cherish the things they own, take pride in them, take care of them? We're not teaching them the best

 a note from
the instructor

BEWARE OF OUTLET MALLS

Too many of us get into trouble at outlet malls. We invest the time to drive to them, so we feel obligated to buy something, even if it's not what we really want or need.

It doesn't matter how low the price; if you don't use it, then it's not a bargain. Instead of falling prey to this kind of emotional buying, make a list of what you truly need before you go shopping, and don't allow yourself to stray from that list.

values. In fact, we're setting them up for a life of clutter, one that is possibly even worse than the one we're struggling with!

WE'RE EMOTIONAL BUYERS

We seem to think that buying something can cure every problem. We think more stuff equals more happiness—and when it doesn't, we assume it's because we don't yet have enough stuff—so back to the store we go.

Advertisers do a tremendous job of convincing us that happiness is just one more purchase away. They tell us in subtle and not-so-subtle ways that if we don't own a particular product, we're less valuable as human beings. Of course, this plays right into our insecurity.

My students occupy a wide range of points on the wealth continuum. You may be surprised to learn that those who earn millions of dollars are no more happy or secure than the middle-class students. I've never

 a note from
the instructor

DON'T FALL FOR "MIRACLE CURE" ORGANIZING PRODUCTS

In order to sell their products, those ingenious marketers will even appeal to your need for order. They'll tell you that you absolutely must have the "right" gadget for organizing, or you'll never get things under control!

It's not that organizing products don't have their place—they do. What's important is to first change your attitude about owning things, and get rid of the excess stuff before you buy any organizing products. Once you have pared down and know what you want to keep and need to store, you can make a decision to use what you have or buy the appropriate product. Again, the important thing is to keep the decisions under your control and make them at the appropriate time. Don't succumb to external pressures to buy.

Yes, there are some terrific organizing products out there, and it's often a blast to shop for them. But don't get caught up in the advertising and the fun of shopping. If you're committed to organizing, you'll often find a way to accomplish it without hauling home more gadgets. And if you're not committed to making the necessary changes, no number of organizing gizmos is going to make any real difference.

seen a direct correlation between a person's number of possessions and their level of happiness. Yet we're "keeping up with the Joneses" like never before. Deep down, we all probably know that possessions don't make us happier or more fulfilled, but in an affluent society like ours, it's easy to forget. We spend too much energy trying to live up to an illusion created by external forces. We're allowing the world around us to take control and dictate the way we should live, rather than letting our individual principles and values guide us.

It's time to step back, define our goals and values, and create the environments that will support them.

WE'RE OFTEN EMOTIONAL *HOARDERS*, TOO

Many of us surround ourselves with clutter for the same reason we overeat: It's a form of protection. Clutter insulates us from the world; it keeps us in a haze of oblivion and excuses that allows us to muffle our pain and anxiety. Clutter and excess body fat are both self-defeating means of protection. Often the underlying issue is loneliness, fear of intimacy, or a need for abundance.

Often people keep things because they're holding on to someone. I have a student who has kept every letter from every boyfriend, even though she says she's actively seeking a new mate. She said, "This is the only way I can remind myself I've been loved." It wasn't until I convinced her to let go of all those keepsakes from the past that she met someone and moved on with her life.

Sometimes people use disorganization to distract themselves from other problems in their lives. Their finances may be in a shambles, so they gloss over it by saying, "I'm just disorganized."

Clutter may come from some "mechanical" dysfunction, like not having enough storage space, the right storage space, or the right tools for organizing. Other underlying causes for clutter are emotional: fear of success, loneliness, loss, or a need for protection.

Is your clutter an excuse to avoid dealing with the real problem in your life? You'll need to answer this honestly before you can deal with your clutter permanently.

If we want to live clutter-free, we must first understand our reasons for clutter.

PEOPLE ARE ALWAYS GIVING US STUFF

Birthdays, Christmas, Hanukkah, bar and bat mitzvahs, anniversaries... every time we turn around, another gift-giving event is coming up. Many people get tremendously stressed out trying to find the right gift. Not everybody's a talented gift-buyer, and few of us have the time to shop as thoughtfully as we'd like. As a result, we don't always do a good job of choosing gifts for others.

Odds are that the prettily wrapped gift we give someone is destined for the bottom of their closet, along with last year's useless gifts—that is, if they'll *fit* in the closet. One of my students once received as a gift a plastic duck the size of a refrigerator!

If people ever find out that you like (or even get the *impression* that you like) a particular animal or symbol, you're doomed! In high school I used to wear a sweater with a rainbow on it, which somehow gave people the impression I was crazy about rainbows. You wouldn't believe the number of rainbow-related things I received over the years. I couldn't make it stop! People would visit my room and say, "Oh, good. Now that I know you like rainbows so much I'll always know what to give you as a present."

How do you turn them down without hurting people's feelings? These gifts are almost always well intentioned, but we simply receive too much stuff to keep and appreciate it all. A friend of mine who received 100 gift baskets when he was ill came up with a wonderful solution: He donated all of them to a homeless shelter.

a note from
the instructor

A COUPLE THOUGHTS ON CREATIVE, CLUTTER-BUSTING GIFTS

I'm an advocate of re-gifting as long as you're careful. If you've ever accidentally re-gifted an unwanted present back to the original giver, you know what I mean!

Consumable gifts like wine or cookies work well as gifts because they don't take up space forever, but give these only if you're sure you know what the person likes. Otherwise, you're still burdening them with another unwanted thing.

Many people express hesitation about giving gift certificates. They fear that the recipient of the certificate will think it's a cop-out. To some, it may seem like the giver couldn't be bothered to put a little effort into finding out what the person likes. I think that's an unfortunate misconception. If you have to give a gift to someone who feels this way, why not give them a gift certificate to their favorite coffee shop, or a store near them that features their favorite hobby?

Gift certificates can be a great way to say, "I know you, and I care enough to know what you like." I once gave a gift certificate from a gourmet cheese shop to a couple who had a passion for cheese.

Services make wonderful gifts and take up no space. How about theater tickets, a day at the spa, or a ride in a hot air balloon?

One of the best gift-giving stories I heard recently was told to me by a couple whose best friends had given them a handmade gift certificate good for an evening of baby-sitting. They went out on the town and had an incredible time. They made a memory that they'll cherish forever, which they'll always associate with their friends, and which will never take up an ounce of space in their closets.

ORGANIZING SEEMS OVERWHELMING

People often put off organizing because they're overwhelmed by the seemingly enormous task, or they're daunted by the prospect of where to start. It's not until they have to face the issue because of some external force, such as moving or expecting a baby, that they take the first step. When they do get started, they find that organizing brings a great deal of instant gratification.

I once had a friend call me in a panic after totaling his car by driving it into a telephone pole. The good news is that he walked away unscathed. Unfortunately, he had misplaced his auto insurance renewal

A donation to a charitable organization can also be a wonderful gift. In choosing a charity, first think about and listen to the recipient of the gift to find out their area of interest. You wouldn't want to make a donation to an animal shelter if your friend has a fear or strong dislike of cats and dogs, but a donation to an art museum could make the perfect gift for a friend who majored in art history and frequents museums every chance she gets.

bill, and his policy had lapsed. That was an expensive wake-up call to the importance of organizing your paperwork.

My students report to me an immediate sense of relief after they've dealt with even a small portion of their clutter. Simple things like cleaning out your wallet or the junk drawer in the kitchen can bring immediate relief.

While some people avoid organizing because it seems like a chore, it's ultimately a matter of attitude. You can make a task more enjoyable by the way you approach it. Turn it into a game, a challenge. Make a party of it: Invite a few friends, turn on great music, and set out snacks.

a note from
the instructor

HOW CAN YOU MOVE FORWARD WHEN CLUTTER IS BLOCKING YOUR PATH?

Having too much clutter and too many items from your past can keep you from moving forward in your life. In these, and many other ways, it can act as a roadblock to accomplishing your goals:

- ■ It's difficult to have clarity about your life or accomplish tasks when you're surrounded by clutter.
- ■ Living in a cluttered environment will sap your energy and lead you to procrastinate.
- ■ Clutter can put your life on hold. I've had students who wanted to relocate but couldn't because of the disarray in their homes. They couldn't put their house on the market in its current state, and the thought of moving to a new home immobilized them.
- ■ Living in chaos can lead to isolation. Many of my students have not had guests in their homes for several years because they're too ashamed.

Do whatever is necessary to get yourself onto the task because the longer you put it off, the worse it's going to get.

WE THINK WE DON'T HAVE THE TIME

We've all used this excuse. We don't have time to organize our lives. We're scrambling as it is just to make time for the essentials! But we all know, whether we want to admit it or not, that streamlining, automating, and organizing our lives will give us *more* time because we won't waste as much of our precious time on unnecessary tasks.

I recommend that you break your decluttering sessions down into smaller tasks. Pick a room and then an area of that room: your bedroom closet, or that awful drawer in the kitchen. While I'd like to be able to tell you it takes three hours to tackle a closet, or one hour to organize a drawer, I can't. The truth is that it takes different people different amounts of time to do things. In addition to working at varying speeds, some people work straight through without distraction, and others take

a note from
the instructor

WHERE DOES ALL THE TIME GO?

- The average person will spend one year searching through desk clutter looking for misplaced objects. —*Margin*, Dr. Richard Swensen

- According to numerous studies, we lose an average of one hour per day searching for misplaced items.

- According to the National Soap and Detergent Association, cleaning professionals say that getting rid of clutter would eliminate 40 percent of the housework in the average home.

- A Gallup Poll found that 50 percent of all Americans claim that they lack enough time to do what they want; 54 percent of parents say they spend too little time with their children; and 47 percent of married couples complain that they lack time together.

time out to answer the phone or deal with family issues. Finally, everyone has their personal comfort level and feels the need to organize to a greater or lesser degree.

To learn how to estimate the length of time it will take you to tackle a particular organizing project, start with some small organizing tasks you have (for instance, a kitchen drawer or single bookshelf). Keep a log to see how long each task takes. After completing a few tasks this way, you will be able to more accurately estimate the time needed to complete future tasks. Once you reach this point, always remember to give yourself a little extra time. It's frustrating to run out of time halfway through a task. If you think the closet will take four hours, then give yourself six. If you simply don't have large chunks of time, tackle small projects that you can complete in the time allotted. It's amazing what you can get done this way if you stay committed to it.

WE RESIST STRUCTURE

Many of us don't like the idea of scheduling our time. We believe that structure will cramp our style and limit our creativity. "It'll take away my freedom!" they lament. I always have the same response: "Your freedom to do what? Spend three hours looking for your keys?"

student experience

"I thought getting organized meant losing my creativity, but now I realize that the opposite is true. When I'm organized, my mind is clear, I'm not as stressed, and I'm more focused. I'll have more energy and time to spend on my passion: photography."
—Nancy, professional photographer

The truth is, it's their disorganization that's robbing them of their creative freedom. People who refuse to get organized for fear it will damage their creativity remain in a state of chaos and disorganization, and *that's* what ultimately restricts their creativity.

Creativity loves organization. When you implement an efficient system tailored to your individual creative needs, you'll find that all your materials are ready at hand and in good condition when inspiration strikes. You'll have the free space to spread out with a new project. Your mind will be clear of distractions, and you'll be able to focus more easily. Organization increases productivity.

One student of mine, an advertising executive who had aspirations of painting but never found the time, told me that after gathering all of her art supplies together and setting up a dedicated space for painting in her home, she began to paint, participated in a regional art show, and sold her first painting.

a note from the instructor

IS WRITER'S BLOCK MADE OF CLUTTER?

A high percentage of my students come from creative fields: musicians, artists, writers, and the like. Many of them express the fear that organizing their lives will rob them of creative freedom, but when they actually get organized, they discover that their creativity is healthier than ever!

The effect is especially profound with writers. Some of my students who write tell me that clutter creates a kind of "noise" in their heads—a serious distraction. Clearing the clutter allows them to take back their concentration.

They also report that organization has the effect of channeling and focusing their creativity. It seems that writer's block is at least partially a result of having unlimited choices. Several writers have told me that it's actually by narrowing the scope of their choices that their creativity finally becomes "concentrated" enough to get them moving again.

It's not hard to see why we're struggling to slay the clutter beast. We've got an awful lot of factors, both physical and emotional, working against us. Now that we've examined some of the causes and hazards of our clutter, let's take a look at a few of the benefits organization offers.

UNCLUTTERING LESSON-END QUESTIONS

Lesson #1:

1. Are you an emotional buyer? Do you regularly shop to:

    ____ cheer yourself when you're depressed?

    ____ calm yourself when you're upset?

    ____ fill a void in your life?

    ____ distract yourself from a problem you should be confronting?

2. If so, describe the events, situations, or emotions that drive you to shop:

    _____

    _____

    _____

3. Do you use your clutter as an excuse to avoid:

    ____ pursuing a relationship?

    ____ taking responsibility for your finances?

    ____ moving your career forward?

4. In the past week, how much time did you spend searching for lost items?

    _____

    _____

    _____

5. Which items do you end up searching for most often?

_____

_____

_____

6. What projects or activities would you be more likely to do if
the objects you needed to do them with were organized and
ready at hand?

_____

_____

_____

_____

_____

_____

the benefits of organizing your life

Organization Saves Time, Reduces Stress, and Saves Money
• Organization Makes You Look Good and Allows You to Get
More Out of Your Home • Organization Is Healthy

In this lesson we discuss the benefits that await you when you make the commitment to organizing your life. As we examine each point, I'd like you to visualize what your life would be like if you were living each aspect of it deliberately, and then contrast it with the way you're living now.

ORGANIZATION SAVES TIME

None of us have more than 24 hours in a day, but we can make our waking hours as productive as possible by being organized. Time management is almost a misnomer, because we can't actually manage *time*. As time-management guru Harold Taylor says, "All we can ever really hope to do is to manage *ourselves* with respect to time."

The key is to plan and prioritize your day. On top of that, you can also arrange your physical environment and train your behaviors so that you can accomplish routine daily tasks with a minimum of time and frustration.

When you get organized, you also cut down on the need to perform unnecessary tasks (searching for the misplaced cell phone, making an extra trip to the store to buy the item you forgot because you didn't make a list, running to your child's school with the forgotten lunch).

Organization streamlines and automates necessary daily tasks, freeing you for more important things. What would you do with more free time? How about spending it with your children, your mate, cherished friends? Or exercise, self-improvement, making more money, or having more fun?

Statistics indicate that we may waste an hour or more per day as a result of disorganization. If you need a tantalizing incentive to get organized, give yourself that daily hour as a gift—think of it as a reward for getting your act together. Decide what you'll do with it and how you'll spend it. Don't just think of it as more padding in case something else takes longer than it should; really invest in that hour and make it something delightful and rejuvenating.

ORGANIZATION REDUCES STRESS

You're already five minutes late, you're headed out the door, and you have no idea where your keys are. A creditor calls to say your monthly payment never arrived, and to your horror, you later discover the missing bill lodged inside your child's invitation to a birthday party (which you forgot to RSVP to). Our possessions have a maddening way of disappearing on us just when we're pressed for time. What a joy it would be to know exactly where to find the things we need when we need them!

One of my students shared with me a recurring conversation she has with her husband: "Honey, do you know where my keys are hiding?" he asks. She replies testily, "They're not *hiding*. They're wherever you put them!" I doubt that those keys actually got up and ran to a hiding place. But when we treat them capriciously, our possessions do seem to act capriciously. When we don't deal with them in a routine fashion and train ourselves to set them down in a designated spot, we can't count on them to be ready for us when we need them next.

a note from
the instructor

WHAT'S CLUTTER COSTING US?

Disorganization could account for as much as 15 to 20 percent of your annual budget: buying duplicates, last-minute shopping at premium prices, finance charges, and late fees on bills.
Stress-related illnesses cost our nation $300 billion annually.

You know what stress does to your mood. It leaves you feeling frazzled, unfocused, and irritable, which is not the best state to be in when dealing with family, friends, and coworkers. It's not a positive way to begin the day, yet across America millions of people launch off each morning into the same frenzied dance.

Rather than living in a constant state of chaos, you can create a calm and orderly environment. Instead of putting yourself in a position of working for your items, you can make the items you need to get through your day work for *you*. The chaos, stress, and frustration that come when you're frantically rounding up necessary items, and searching for misplaced ones, is completely voluntary. You can choose to avoid it by getting organized.

ORGANIZATION SAVES MONEY AND HELPS YOU MAKE MORE

A shipshape household wastes less food, needs to replace appliances and furnishings far less often (because they're maintained better), and makes more efficient use of nearly everything it has. It also reduces distractions so that you can become more productive and focused. You'll work more effectively, and this will translate into creating more wealth.

We probably have no real idea how much money disorganization costs us because we seldom have the time to stop and add it all up. One thing is certain: The cost is cumulative and can snowball into a massive sum of money.

For example, a friend's wife neglected to check the oil in her car regularly, which caused the engine to seize (that's at least $2,000 right

a note from
the instructor

MOVING?

It's the most common lament I hear from people who've recently moved: "Why in the world did I think this stuff was important enough to move all the way across town (or across the country)?"

That's a good question, especially when you consider that a lot of moving companies today charge by the pound. It's not uncommon for the weight of a very modest group of household items, like that of a single person living in a one-room apartment, to top 3,000 pounds!

How much of your stuff—particularly those items you haven't looked at or touched in five years—are really worth paying a $1 a pound and up just to cart with you into your new home where, odds are, they'll continue to sit unused?

there for a new engine). She also had to pay to have the vehicle towed and then stored while it sat waiting for its new engine. Meanwhile, the wife took the husband's SUV to work.

The husband remembered an appointment only after the wife had taken the vehicle. He would have called a friend to ask for a ride, but his cell phone (the only place he kept the friend's phone number) was in the glove compartment of—you guessed it—his SUV. So he was forced to take a cab instead, which cost him $14 each way.

When the cab dropped him off that evening, he couldn't get into the house because it was locked and his wife had his keys. So he had to break a window to get back into his own home. At the end of the day, the couple had incurred nearly $3,000 of unplanned (and avoidable) expenses! When our lives are in order, we have far fewer unexpected expenses and far more time and energy to focus on earning our income.

ORGANIZATION MAKES A BETTER IMPRESSION

Your guests and business associates will form a better opinion of you if your house and office are clean, clutter-free, and aesthetically pleasing, and this effect is exponential if you're showing your home to potential buyers!

a note from the instructor

WANT TO GET TOP DOLLAR WHEN YOU SELL YOUR HOME?

Before you spend thousands of dollars renovating, consider clearing out your clutter as a preliminary step toward getting your house on the market. Realtors regard "first impression" improvements such as decluttering closets as one of the smartest ways to speed the sale of a home and get a better price. Think of it this way: You'll have to deal with that clutter when your house sells anyway; why not do it now, so that you can maximize your chances of getting top dollar?

The condition of your surroundings is a reflection of your internal state. How do you want to represent yourself? Does your home or office take away your credibility? Your home often represents what's going on inside you. Are you feeling out of control?

ORGANIZATION ENABLES YOU TO GET MORE ENJOYMENT OUT OF YOUR HOME

One couple, whose apartment I organized, discovered to their astonishment that they had been eating at restaurants every day for the past four years because their kitchen and dining room had become buried under mounds of unappetizing clutter. They were paying an enormous mortgage each month for rooms that basically functioned as holding tanks for their unused possessions. And that was on top of the cost of eating out three times a day, 365 days a year.

With the cost of real estate these days, shouldn't our homes be more than extremely expensive storage units for our clutter?

In today's world, people feel more vulnerable and less in control. It's more important than ever for us to create a safe, calm, beautiful environment in our homes so that we have a retreat when we need to rest and recharge. The world outside our door is frantic enough; if our homes also produce stress, where can we go to nourish our need for calm, order, and beauty?

You'll feel more relaxed and nurtured in a house that's comfortably tidy and in good order. Cooking will become a joy instead of a frustration. You'll be able to savor a good book without the distraction of out-of-control clutter. You'll take more pride in your artwork, furnishings, and collections because mounds of accumulated junk won't obscure them. If your clutter is bad enough, you might have even stopped inviting friends to your house. Imagine, instead, welcoming them in with confidence to a home that's your pride and joy.

ORGANIZATION MAY EVEN IMPROVE YOUR HEALTH

Ancient Chinese wisdom has it that your house is an extension of your body, and that the state of your home represents the state of your health. Science backs this up: The best environment for good health is a clean, tidy, well-ventilated, well-lit home—in short, the antithesis of clutter.

We've talked about the tension, frustration, and anxiety disorganization causes. I'm not a doctor, but I'm sure you don't need me to tell you how many modern illnesses have been linked to stress.

Additionally, if you're really, truly disorganized, you're probably missing out on regular doctor's exams, and you're unlikely to be able to commit to a regular fitness routine.

I know you've heard that there are good and bad kinds of stress, but I'm here to tell you that the stress inflicted by disorganization doesn't do anybody any good! If you're looking for beneficial stress, go out and

 a note from the instructor

BENEFITS OF STRESS REDUCTION

Reducing clutter reduces stress. What can reduced stress do for you? Numerous studies indicate that cutting down on stress:

- Enhances mental focus.
- Promotes more restful sleep.
- Improves the immune system.
- May lower blood pressure.
- May prevent illness.

challenge yourself. Go back to school, get into a new sport, go work with disadvantaged teenagers. Whatever you do, though, don't subject yourself to the kind of stress that simply grinds away at your soul a little every day and gives you nothing in return.

Imagine living in a home and working in a space that radiates a sense of well-being. Everything's clean, orderly, well-lit, in good repair, and pleasing to the eye. Remember that these two places are where you'll spend the vast majority of your life. Home and work environments have an enormous effect on your mood and health. You owe it to yourself to create an environment that calms and energizes you, that minimizes stress and maximizes your efforts to maintain good health.

By now I hope I've convinced you of the detriments of clutter and the enormous benefits of organizing your life. Now it's time to get personal. We're going to take a closer look at your own unique brand of disorganization as we begin to lay the foundation for transforming your life.

UNCLUTTERING LESSON-END QUESTIONS

Lesson #2:

1. Which items do you misplace most often?

_____

_____

_____

_____

_____

2. How much time would you estimate you spend each week searching for misplaced items?

_____

_____

_____

_____

_____

3. What would you do with the extra time you listed in Question 1, if you didn't have to spend it searching for lost items?

_____

_____

_____

_____

_____

4. List some of the ways disorganization costs you money; for instance, having to pay overdue library fines, late fees on bills, buying forgotten grocery items at convenience stores, paying for preventable car repairs, and so forth. Try to assign a dollar amount to each item you list. Total this amount.

_____

_____

_____

_____

_____

5. Go through your checkbook register and other financial records, and mark with a star all expenses for the past month that were a result of disorganization. Total this amount.

_____

_____

_____

_____

_____

6. Look at the figures you came up with in Questions 4 and 5. How would you have preferred to spend this money if you had not spent it on disorganization?

_____

_____

_____

_____

_____

Other Thoughts:

_____

_____

_____

_____

_____

_____

assess your mess

Give Yourself an Early Victory • Nine Steps
to an Uncluttered Life

Organizing is a highly personal process. There are many ways to organize your belongings, and one method is not inherently better than another. What matters most is which organizing system works best for you. As you begin the organizing process, it becomes critical for you to assess your needs and determine your desired lifestyle. Then organize your time and space in a way that best supports the way you wish to live.

GIVE YOURSELF AN EARLY VICTORY

If you're like many people, you've first got to break through a virtual wall of resistance to get to a point where you're ready to declutter. You'll find that wall a lot easier to negotiate if you're truly convinced of the rewards that await you on the other side. That's why I'd like you to start off with a success. It will be a small one, but it will give you a taste of what's to come.

Start with the area that's causing you the most stress. Which room bothers you the most? Within that room, which area? Within that area, which portion? Break the job down into small increments so that it won't seem like such an overwhelming process. You might be left with just a single shelf in a closet—that's fine for now. Even by tackling one small area, you'll start to experience immediate rewards and begin to get an idea of what the overall effort will entail. Do it now!

STEP 1: IDENTIFY YOUR INDIVIDUAL ORGANIZATION NEEDS

Your goal here is to recognize your individual and household needs so that you can organize in a way that keeps your house clutter-free. You don't want your home to have a sterile feeling, but it must be organized and clean. Remember, your environment is a direct reflection of you, and you want to present yourself in the best way possible.

Each household's requirements are different. Do you need to have tools, suitcases, or reference materials ready at hand? Could you use an entire closet devoted to pet paraphernalia? Do you entertain often enough that you need fresh linen and good china at the ready, or could they be packed away for the once or twice a year you actually use it?

STEP 2: MAKE A PLAN

While it's important to have a strong sense of all of the activities you wish to conduct in your home, you should focus on one room, or one area, at a time. I suggest that you begin with the room that's causing you the most stress. As you assess the room, you need to determine what "macro" activities will be served there: food preparation, sewing, studying, etc. You don't need to plan the entire house before you begin decluttering; you can take this one room at a time.

Make a floor plan for that room and mark the activities that take place there. Then plan "micro" areas for each activity: packing kids' lunches, sewing leather items, reading general reference materials, and so forth. Design the type of storage each area requires; do this with an eye toward making it harmonize with the overall appearance of the room. We'll get into specific storage ideas and organizational strategies in later lessons, but for now I want you to concentrate on grouping the items that you need for each task and finding ways to make performing those activities as problem-free as possible.

a note from
the instructor

STORAGE AREAS YOU MIGHT NOT HAVE THOUGHT OF

- Benches and stools with built-in storage.
- Areas above doors and windows.
- Areas beneath cabinets (for hanging items).
- Nonfunctioning fireplaces.
- Nooks under stairways.

You'll have to work at implementing new habits, but remember that the systems you create must make sense to you. They shouldn't be too complex. Storage should correspond to the place the object is used. If you have a coat closet clear across the room from your main entrance, you can be assured that coats will land anywhere and everywhere. One solution to this dilemma is to place a coat rack near the door. More practical yet, put a row of hooks on the wall near the entrance.

STEP 3: GET RID OF THE CLUTTER

Anything that you're not using or enjoying is clutter. Get it out of your life! You can't enjoy the benefits of organization until you've gotten rid of the stuff that, by its very nature, creates chaos and wastes your time.

As you move through the room, you're going to make a decision about each item. I teach my students to use the "sorting box" technique when they get to this step:

1. Get five large boxes and park them in front of the closet, room, or area you're decluttering.

2. Mark your boxes as follows: #1 is for items to throw away, #2 for donation to charity, #3 to give to family and friends (this includes that staggering number of objects in your house that you've been meaning to give back to their owners),

#4 objects that need repair, and #5 objects that belong in another room or area.

3. Sort all the objects in the targeted area into these boxes. Items you want to keep that actually belong in that spot can go back in to await your new organizing system (which we'll get to shortly). Now is the time to decide the fate of each item. With every object you pick up, ask yourself these questions:

- When was the last time I used this item?

- Do I need this many?

- Is it beautiful?

- If I got rid of it and then needed it, would it be difficult to get another? What would be the *worst* that could happen?

- What is it costing me to maintain and store this item?

Many of my students find this process frustrating and difficult. They're frightened of letting go of so many of their possessions, especially all at once. When someone's really suffering at this stage, I sometimes suggest that they use a sixth sorting box labeled "undecided." When the sorting is done, we tape the undecided box shut, write the date on it, and put it away for exactly a year with the agreement that if the student hasn't needed any item in the box within that time, out it goes without another glance at the contents.

STEP 4: INVENTORY WHAT YOU OWN

Now that you've rid yourself of the bulk of your clutter, it's time to take inventory of the items you've decided to keep. Often when I get to this step with my students, their eyes go wide and they ask, "You mean I have to go through *everything* I've decided to keep?" Yes, everything. You're now going to become a conscious owner because you can't maintain control over things you don't know you have. This step sounds painful and time consuming, but it's an eye-opener. Trust me.

In fact, once you've pared everything down to what you're going to keep, I want you to write down a list of what you're keeping. There's something about committing it to paper that reveals where your choices aren't making a lot of sense.

Start by sorting items into categories. This will make it easier to assess what you have and determine what you need. The goal here is to keep only those items that you use and love. Anything *not* used or loved is, by definition, clutter.

student experience

"I never thought of taking inventory and sorting all my possessions into categories to determine exactly what and how much of everything you own. Now that I've gone through the process, I realize that it really was the first step to taking control of my possessions rather than having my possessions control me. I was able to make better decisions about what I wanted to keep and what I was ready to get rid of."

—Lisa, mâitre d'

STEP 5: TAKE STOCK OF YOUR HOME'S STORAGE

Now that you've inventoried your possessions and know what you have to store, look at your house, make a mental note of existing storage areas, and list places that could be modified for additional storage. Look for corners, spaces above doorways, and any other areas that could accommodate additional storage. At this point, it's important that you either identify existing storage or create new storage to accommodate the possessions that you need to house in your available space.

Whenever my students complain that they don't have room to store anything, I tell them to go home, lie on the floor, and look up. See all that empty space up there? Use it! Install shelves above doorways and windows, install hooks for items that can live in hanging baskets, lay storage platforms across open beams. Get creative. Don't let all that space go to waste!

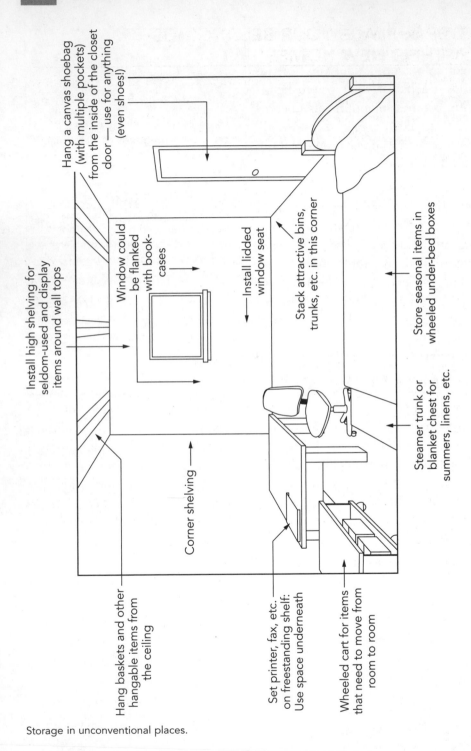

Hang a canvas shoebag
(with multiple pockets)
from the inside of the closet
door — use for anything
(even shoes!)

Install high shelving for
seldom-used and display
items around wall tops

Window could
be flanked
with book-
cases

Install lidded
window seat

Stack attractive bins,
trunks, etc. in this corner

Store seasonal items in
wheeled under-bed boxes

Steamer trunk or
blanket chest for
summers, linens, etc.

Corner shelving

Hang baskets and other
hangable items from
the ceiling

Set printer, fax, etc.
on freestanding shelf:
Use space underneath

Wheeled cart for items
that need to move from
room to room

Storage in unconventional places.

STEP 6: PLACE YOUR BELONGINGS IN THEIR NEW HOMES

Now that you've identified the items that you wish to keep and have located or created appropriate storage, it's time to assign your belongings to their new homes. This is a gratifying part of the organizing process, and students often report feeling an immediate sense of calm at this point.

STEP 7: IDENTIFY YOUR CLUTTER PATTERNS

Once you've decluttered, you'll be able to observe your behavior and determine if there are remaining problems you need to address. Now it's time to identify those remaining problem areas in your home and workspaces. Are there areas that continue to accumulate clutter? Make a list of each problem area and describe the type of clutter that accumulates there. You may find it helpful to draw a layout of your home and mark each area where clutter collects. This will help you target the cause of the clutter and identify potential solutions.

The following list is what I call "The Dirty Dozen": 12 chronic clutter areas in the average home. Check these locations in your own home to make sure you've identified all the places that your clutter is piling up:

1. Kitchen utensil drawers.
2. Catch-all "hell" drawers.
3. Kitchen countertops.
4. Wherever paperwork waits to be filed.
5. Bathroom medicine cabinets.
6. Under beds.
7. Closets.
8. Cabinets.
9. Basements.
10. Attics.
11. Garages.
12. Desk drawers.

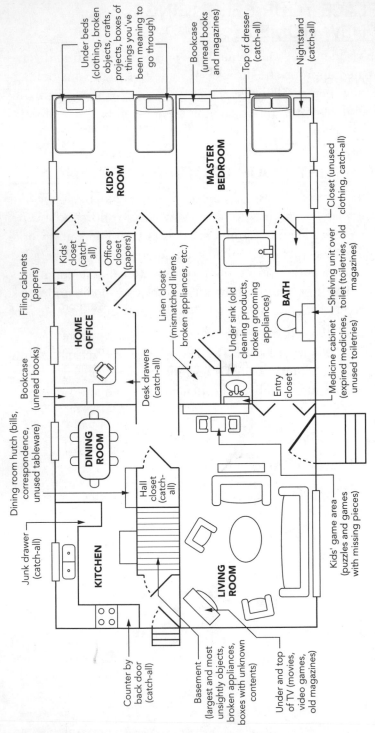

Schematic of a home with clutter-prone areas identified.

a note from
the instructor

TYPES OF CLUTTER AND WHAT YOU CAN DO ABOUT THEM

Inherited/Heirloom: Clutter you inherited from family members. You don't have to keep it. If you don't love it, or if it's not useful, pass it along to someone who wants it. If it does have some meaning but it's too unwieldy to keep, take a photo of it and keep a scrapbook of pictures to remind you of the item after you've given it away.

Gifts: There's no rule that says if someone gave you something, you're obligated to keep it forever. If it really doesn't fit into your life long term, why not enjoy it a few times, perhaps with the person who gave it to you, and then let it find a new home?

Broken Items: Ask yourself how much time and money it will take to fix them, and evaluate honestly whether it's really worth your time. If the answer is yes, estimate a time when you can actually commit to fixing the objects. If you don't do it during the allotted time, the items were probably not important enough for you to fix. Get rid of them.

Collections: Do you truly gain pleasure from them in relation to the time and money it's costing you to maintain them? If you want to maximize the pleasure you're getting from your collection, display it prominently. If it's always tucked away in a box somewhere, what's the point of collecting?

"Maybe someday" items: Objects that you have no current use for but you keep just in case. How often have you needed it in the past year? How much space is it taking up? How expensive or difficult would it be to replace it if you got rid of it but needed one again? This can sometimes be a tough call. As a general rule, though, get rid of most of these kinds of "just in case" items unless they really might be needed some day and are hard to come by.

Sunken cost clutter: Items you don't like but spent good money on, so you feel obligated to keep. Let them go. As long as you keep them, they will continue to cost you. Cut your losses and move on.

Bargain items: These are also sunken cost clutter, only cheaper: items that were bought on sale but were never quite right. Treat them the same way. Let them go.

STEP 8: CATCH YOURSELF IN THE ACT

Now that you're becoming conscious of your clutter patterns, I'd like you to pay particular attention to your own behavior. What do you do that contributes to the clutter? Think of your behavior analytically in much the same way you just assessed your house. Identify the times, circumstances, even the moods, that leave you prone to creating clutter.

student experience

"My house was always very clean, but I still couldn't find anything. OK, so being neat is not the same thing as being organized."
—David, network administrator

In time you're going to choose new behaviors and retrain yourself to handle that particular task in a more orderly way, but be gentle with yourself. Remember that everyone has different needs. It's your home: Modify it to the way you prefer to do things. This will make it a lot easier to adapt to the changes, which means you're far more likely to enjoy lasting success in your organizing efforts.

STEP 9: RETRAIN YOURSELF

Once your clutter is gone and your organization system is in place, and you have a heightened awareness of your own spatial and behavioral problem areas, you'll learn to adapt to this new way of doing things. This is simply a matter of time, commitment, and patience. Just as with any change in behaviors, you'll slip up from time to time. That's okay. Just make sure that when you fall, you get back on the horse as quickly as possible.

Be gentle with yourself: It's not easy to change habits and behaviors of this magnitude. Give yourself time to get used to the new systems, but revise them if you feel as though you're fighting the tide all the time. All of us have our individual quirks: We should accommodate them where we can.

UNCLUTTERING LESSON-END QUESTIONS

Lesson #3:

1. What single clutter-prone area in your home (for instance, a closet, drawer, shelf, or corner) causes you the most stress, and why?

_____

_____

_____

2. Once you've decluttered and organized this area, describe how you feel.

_____

_____

_____

3. What specific organizing needs do you have? List hobbies, work tools and supplies, reading habits, and so forth.

_____

_____

_____

4. Rank all the rooms and other areas of your home from most to least clutter-prone (you can use this list to tell you the order in which to tackle each area).

Other Thoughts:

_____

_____

_____

_____

_____

_____

principles of clutter-free living

Commit to Being Organized • If It's Not Essential, Let It Go •
A Place for Everything and Everything in Its Place •
The Power of To-Do Lists

The sooner you become organized, the longer you'll have to benefit from your efforts. So go ahead, make the commitment to an organized lifestyle and be on your way to a more productive and stress-free life. While I recognize that becoming organized will take a dedicated time commitment, once you're organized there are several quick and easy tools you can use to help maintain order in your life. In this lesson we'll explore some of the time-tested tools that will help you to live free of clutter.

MAKE IT A COMMITMENT

I'd like you to think of this new change toward organization as a commitment to a whole new lifestyle. Change is scary for many of us, and a large-scale commitment like this is daunting to nearly everyone. So be

a note from
the instructor

BUT I HAVE THE ROOM. . .

Whenever students tell me they don't need to declutter because they have plenty of room for storage, I point out that unwanted possessions occupy far more than physical space. Keeping belongings that you no longer use still weighs on you. They're taking up space in your psyche, even if they're tucked away where you don't see them. Out of sight isn't really out of mind.

gentle on yourself. Recognize that change is a process, and give yourself time. Remember, psychologists claim that it takes a minimum of 21 days for a new habit to take hold. Give yourself *at least* that much time.

It's not easy, but you *can* do it. It's difficult to transform years of clutter-producing habits, but if you stick with it long enough to allow this new way of living to become routine, you'll make a miraculous discovery: *It's a lot easier to live without clutter than it was to live with it!*

Take Your Commitment Seriously

I meant it when I said you need to think of this as a whole-life commitment. Think of the most profound commitments you've made in your life—the ones you've stuck to, the ones that are a source of pride. Have you successfully lost weight, run a marathon, or quit smoking? If you're happily married, or sincerely committed to your faith, you know what it's like to be committed to something with your mind, heart, and body. Make a commitment on this level to live a clutter-free life, strive to return to it even when you slip up, and you *will* succeed.

Living Clutter-Free Has Broad Implications

For many of us, just doing it for ourselves isn't enough to cement the commitment. When we do it for something bigger than ourselves, we often find that a powerful new wind has filled our sails. So vow to make this change for the biggest reasons you can think of: to set a good example for your kids, to free up more time to be with loved ones, to become more effective in your life's work, to liberate yourself from "thing-itis" in order to live a more spiritual life. Find whatever is most meaningful to you and use it to change your life for the better.

Invest the Time Now; Enjoy the Returns Forever

It will take time, initially, to transform your home into a clutter-free, well-oiled machine, just as it will take time to teach yourself new organizing habits. Think of it as an investment. You'll begin enjoying the returns immediately, and they'll last you a lifetime.

HOW ORGANIZED DO YOU NEED TO BE?

If you're prone to excessive behavior, beware. Organizing and tidiness, like exercising, collecting, or half a dozen other things, can become an obsession for some people. I want you to get your life in order, but I don't want you to become an organization maniac. Remember that it's a means to an end, not an end in and of itself.

So don't go overboard. Don't become what a friend calls "nasty neat," and leave the plastic slipcovers on your couches even when company comes over. You don't need to exchange one set of unproductive behaviors for another. But you *do* need to be organized enough that

 a note from
the instructor

NOT THE LEGACY YOU WANT TO LEAVE

If you're still not convinced it's worth the effort to organize your life and deal with your junk, I'd like to offer a sobering reminder. Do you know that when the average person dies, they leave behind an enormous chore for their next of kin to deal with? Grieving relatives find themselves saddled with sorting through a lifetime of accumulated clutter, a task that can rob them of many precious days, weeks, or even months.

A student shared the following experience: When her grandfather died last year, she discovered that he had left all of his possessions in perfect order. By living an organized life and having everything under control, he'd left his family a final gift. They were able to mourn his death and celebrate his life without the added burden of sorting through mounds of useless clutter. In actuality, he had given two gifts to his family: the gift of comfort (knowing that he had taken care of everything) and the gift of time.

you're not frantic, sloppy, unable to keep what you have in good condition, or unable to find what you need. You only need to organize to a level that is comfortable for you, one you can learn to maintain easily.

Toss the Old One When You Get a New One

I know how the thinking goes: "My DVD player is old and not as good as the ones they're making today. I'll get a new one for the living room and keep the old one around in case the new one breaks." Then the old one sits on a shelf collecting dust, never to play another movie.

Now that you have a new DVD player (coffee maker, computer, stereo, hairdryer) when are you ever going to get around to using the old one? Toss it; or better yet, donate it to charity.

student experience

"I never knew how long to keep my old record albums or even which ones to keep. When I did some research on which records were really valuable, I found that I could throw away all but a few boxes of what I'd been hoarding. I gained tons of space in my attic."
—Jodi, salesperson

Reduce Paper

Paper is one of the worst clutter offenders. No other type of clutter consumes as much time. A client of mine actually rented a storage unit for decades to do nothing else but hold boxes of her ancient paperwork. She hadn't looked at any of it in years! Yet every time she moved, she had to pay to have it shipped. She also had to find a new storage unit for all the paper to rot in. Paper can get out of hand quickly, and when it does, it can gobble space and time like nothing else.

Once you've tackled your backlog, your best defense against paper clutter is to never let it get ahead of you again. Cut it out wherever you can. Pay bills online. Convert to e-mail. Save records on disk. Keep only the past year's vital records close at hand; store the previous seven years' paperwork in a box in long-term storage. Throw away the rest.

Cancel Most Magazine and Newspaper Subscriptions

Too many people I know subscribe to so many magazines that they can't even name all their subscriptions. These people often lack the time to read the magazine once it arrives, and then they feel guilty that they paid for it and didn't "get to it" yet. So once it makes its way into their house, it takes up permanent residence.

My advice to magazine-lovers is to peruse the issue quickly the moment it arrives. Mark the articles you have a genuine interest in reading. Read them as soon as you can, clip the articles that are worth keeping, and then throw the magazine away. Better yet, donate old magazines to a doctor's office or shelter. If you seldom read them, don't have them taking up space in your home. Cancel your subscription, and when you really want a particular issue, buy it from your local newsstand or enjoy it for free at your public library. If you have a friend who subscribes to similar types of magazines, cancel some of yours and swap with him.

Never Set Junk Mail Down

Don't give it a chance to accumulate! Keep a trashcan handy where you gather mail or where you enter your home. Toss the unwanted stuff into the trash as soon as you pick up the mail.

Someone once told me about a coworker who so detested all the advertisements that came in his monthly bills that he enclosed them in the return envelope when he wrote out his check and mailed them back to the company. I'm not advocating that you do that, but if you're really drowning in the stuff, see Lesson 15 for places you can write or call to get your name off solicitation lists.

A PLACE FOR EVERYTHING AND EVERYTHING IN ITS PLACE

It may sound like a trite old axiom, but it's stuck around all these years because it works. This should be the governing principle in your organizational scheme. Everything you're keeping needs to have a place to live. Keeping your space in order will be mostly a matter of returning all items, in good condition, to their designated places. There's another benefit, too: When each item has its own place, you know right where to look when you need it.

NEVER LET IT GET OUT OF CONTROL

It's heartbreaking to invest hours and days of your life organizing, only to have your home revert to its original cluttered state seemingly overnight. The only way to prevent this is to stay on top of your organizing routines at all times:

- **Organize from the beginning:** When you move to a new house, start a new hobby, or buy a new collection, train yourself to buy, build, or improvise an organizational system for it from the beginning.

  Just moving in? This is a great time to make the change to an organized lifestyle. Edit your possessions and take inventory before you move. You'll probably save 10% or more on the cost of moving. Best of all, this allows you to start out fresh in your new home with only the essentials.

  Before you bring in your possessions, scour your new home for storage possibilities. Look for places that could accommodate some of those innovative storage ideas you've been brainstorming. If you need to create the storage space, tackle that task before you move in; then you'll be able to store your possessions right away and begin your clutter-free life.

  Got a new fish tank? Before you even bring it home, get a cabinet for the tank to stand on with plenty of drawers and shelves for the fish paraphernalia.

- **The 10-Minute-A-Day Rule:** Your new organizing systems won't work for long unless you're equally committed to maintaining them. Now that all your possessions serve your goals, and each item has a place of its own, set aside 10 minutes each day to return all items to their places. It's not that hard to find 10 minutes, even on the busiest day, but it's almost impossible to find the several hours or more you'll need if you allow a little untidiness to turn back into a monster.

  Take your 10 minutes whenever they fit your particular schedule. Go from room to room, returning everything to its place. Keep a bin for items that belong in other rooms; drop items into this bin throughout the day, and then whisk them back to their places in their proper room during your 10-minute blitz.

- **Automate wherever you can:** Automate your daily tasks; set up shortcuts wherever possible. Keep your grocery list in a file on the computer. Each time you go to the store, add any additional items you need to the basic weekly list, print it out, and go. Do the same with the list for the baby-sitter, chores for the kids, and so forth.

- **Group related items:** You'll significantly reduce travel time and frustration if you put all items of a type together. In the kitchen, store coffee, filters, sugar, and creamer together near the coffee pot. Have a tray of ketchup, mustard, barbecue sauce, and so forth in a caddy ready to go to the dinner table or outside for a barbecue.

Keep an index card box of business cards for local services and store it, along with yellow and white pages, an address book, and pens and note paper, within arm's reach of the phone. Store hats, gloves, and scarves in the same place you keep coats. You'd be amazed at the mileage you can log traveling from room to room if all these items are kept in different locations! Keep all cleaning supplies together in a caddy that can easily travel with you from room to room as you clean.

MAKE TO-DO LISTS

I'm a great advocate of the to-do list. When you handle these lists efficiently, they can streamline your daily tasks and keep chores and appointments from slipping between the cracks.

The real trick to making lists work for you is to keep them all in one place. Some of my clients have lists hidden all over the house—they can never find them when they need them! Keep a single, prioritized, master to-do list, and organize your daily to-do lists from it. Then turn to your calendar and schedule your tasks according to your own unique way of doing things: If your highest energy level is early in the morning, schedule tasks that require the most clarity and effort first thing. If lunch makes you sleepy, and you drag your way through the afternoons—as many of us do—schedule the tasks requiring the least brainpower for the afternoon hours.

Tackle your list in whatever way works best for you. Some people prefer to do the fastest and easiest thing on the list first; they save the

a note from
the instructor

BUT THEY LOOK SO USEFUL! THE HAZARDS OF SELF-STICKING NOTES

Who doesn't love those little self-sticking notes? Just having them sitting on your desk can make you feel more organized, and if you use them properly, they can be a boon to your work. But self-sticking notes have an insidious habit that can undo your most sincere efforts: They migrate.

If you don't keep a tight rein on those little devils, they'll find their way all over the house. They'll cover your computer screen, they'll leap at you from the refrigerator door when you reach for the milk, they'll stick to the back of your dress when you're doing a business presentation (yes, *that's* what they were all snickering at).

One of my clients became nearly frantic when she couldn't find the one self-sticking note that carried the information she desperately needed. She called me days later to relate, "You wouldn't believe where I found it—in the medicine cabinet!"

By all means, if they work for you, then use them. But be forewarned. Designate a place for them to hang, use them sparingly in datebooks, and don't permit them to sneak off to parts unknown.

hardest for last so that they can use the momentum of accomplishment to carry them through the rest. Others would rather take on the most daunting task first because that's when they have the most energy.

Write down items you need when you first notice you need them. Laminate and hang lists that remain the same from week to week, like household chores for various members of the family, kids' activity schedules, and so forth. Organize shopping lists by the layout of the store; organize shopping trips by their geographic location.

There are two additional benefits to using to-do lists: Once a task goes on the list, you can let it out of your head, and crossing a completed task off your list is very satisfying. Try it and see!

UNCLUTTERING LESSON-END QUESTIONS

Lesson #4:

1. Describe here a commitment you've made and stuck with—one you're proud of (for instance, your marriage vow or a weight-loss regimen). Describe the reward and satisfaction you've enjoyed as a result of sticking with it.

_____

_____

_____

2. Now describe what it might be like to make that same level of commitment to being organized. Describe in detail the rewards you would receive and the pride you'd feel.

_____

_____

_____

Other Thoughts:

_____

_____

_____

_____

_____

_____

keep it, refurbish it, or throw it away?

Paperwork and Filing Systems • Dealing with Books, Magazines, Videos, and Other Media • Games and Toys • Photos • Three Ways to Get Rid of Your Junk

Clutter takes on a bewildering array of forms. Most homes suffer from several types of clutter, each with its own causes and organizing issues. In this lesson we'll take a look at some of the most common household offenders and examine a few of the reasons they tend to create clutter. Then I'll offer solutions that will guide you in managing and getting rid of your clutter.

PAPER

One of the top clutter disasters in homes and offices is paper. In spite of the movement in recent years to digitize and store documents and images on computers, we continue to bury ourselves in an avalanche of

45

paper. Here, more than in practically any other area, we let ourselves get spooked by the I-might-need-it-someday goblin.

I want to address that fear on two fronts. First, the odds that you'll actually refer to a given document again are about one-in-five. With some discernment you can choose the documents with higher odds (tax and accounting paperwork, legal documents, and bank statements, for instance) and pitch the ones that have almost zero chance (the church bulletin from last February). You can head off a good 50 to 70 percent of that particular anxiety by developing a sense of what you actually do need to keep. More on that in a minute.

Second, since the chances are so slim that you'll ever retrieve a given piece of information, you could choose not to keep it yourself and simply use the library or Internet when you need it. A great deal of the information that people hold on to (health news, for instance) soon becomes obsolete. If a health issue does arise, you'll want the most up-to-date information. Don't waste valuable space and time storing documents that you'll probably never reference again.

We often allow ourselves to become inundated with paperwork because we don't keep up with it on a regular basis. Paperwork maintenance follows the same rule as most other chores: If you do it once per month, it's a two-hour project; if you do it once a day, it takes five minutes or less. Which is easier for you to find: five minutes or two *hours?*

If you're going to stay ahead of paperwork, it has to be part of your routine. You must schedule a specific time to do it or it won't get done.

Action Files:
Items requiring
action

Desktop hanging
file system

Reference Materials:
Information that may
be difficult to replace

2-drawer filing cabinet

Everything Else

Wastebasket or
paper recycling bin

Handling paperwork.

Creating a System to Handle Your Paperwork

Not only do you need to have a designated time scheduled to process your paperwork, you also need to designate an area in your house as the home-management center.

Now that you're sitting down at the designated time and in the designated space to process your paperwork, it's decision-making time. What should you keep and what should you throw away? With each piece of paper you process, ask yourself three things:

1. Do I need to take any action as a result of this incoming information?

2. Should I file it as reference material?

3. What's the worst that will happen if I toss it, and can I live with that?

Once you have sorted all your paperwork, you'll need to create two different sets of files. One set will be your action files, the other your reference files.

Action Files

For your action files, I suggest a desktop filing system that will hold letter-size hanging files with inserts. You want your action files to be extremely accessible. Choose a file and label color that you like, and create a set of action files that meets your specific needs—you might include these categories:

- To Act
- To Buy
- To Call
- To Pay
- To Schedule
- To Send

You may also want a file designated for each family member in your desktop filing system; this way you'll have a place to put any papers that they may need to review or act on.

Reference Files

For your reference files you'll need a filing cabinet that will house your reference materials in letter-size hanging files (a two-drawer filing cabinet seems to be sufficient for most people, but you'll need to measure that for yourself).

Choose a color for these files that is different from the one you chose for your action files. The hanging files should be labeled by category, and insert files should be placed inside the hanging files and labeled with the appropriate category and/or subcategory.

File reference material by category. Designate and label a hanging file for each broad category of information; for instance:

- Entertainment
- Financial
- Fitness
- Gift ideas
- Health
- Insurance
- Interior Design
- Manuals/Warranties
- Medical
- School
- Taxes
- Travel

Within each of these broad category files you can insert subcategory files. For example, in your Insurance file, you might include subcategory files such as:

- Insurance/Automobile
- Insurance/Health
- Insurance/Life
- Insurance/Homeowner's

If you work at home, keep a separate set of both action and reference files for your business materials. Choose two different colors for these categories so that you can distinguish them from your personal files.

How to Handle Bills

For bills, use your action file marked "To Pay," and place insert files labeled Week 1, Week 2, Week 3, Week 4, and Week 5. When you receive a bill, file it a few days before the due date to allow for mail time. Each week when you're processing your paper, pull out the files that correspond to that week and pay bills for that time period. You can then place the bills to be mailed in an area designated for outgoing mail. Make sure that the outgoing mail actually goes out on a daily basis.

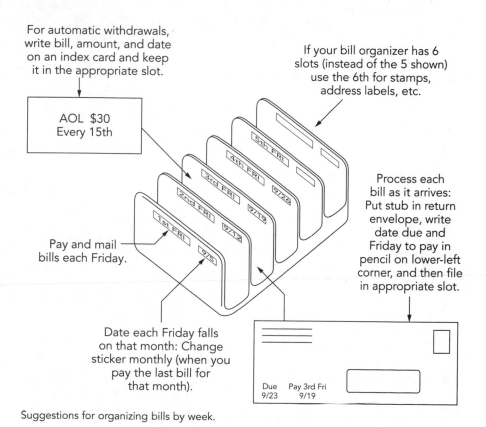

For automatic withdrawals, write bill, amount, and date on an index card and keep it in the appropriate slot.

AOL $30
Every 15th

If your bill organizer has 6 slots (instead of the 5 shown) use the 6th for stamps, address labels, etc.

5th FRI

4th FRI   9/26

3rd FRI   9/19

2nd FRI   9/12

1st FRI   9/5

Pay and mail bills each Friday.

Process each bill as it arrives: Put stub in return envelope, write date due and Friday to pay in pencil on lower-left corner, and then file in appropriate slot.

Date each Friday falls on that month: Change sticker monthly (when you pay the last bill for that month).

Due   Pay 3rd Fri
9/23   9/19

Suggestions for organizing bills by week.

It takes less than 10 extra seconds to sort bills by week, and the time you spend could save you endless hours of agony searching for the lost bill. More importantly, this system can help you avoid expensive late fees and the loss of your financial reputation if you permit lost, overdue bills to ruin your credit!

How to Handle Legal Documents

When it comes to legal or financial documents, check with your accountant and/or attorney to determine what you need to keep. You only need to keep records for the current year and the previous year close at hand, unless you're applying for a mortgage or other big-ticket credit item. Put the rest in long-term storage. Keep records of recent bill and credit payments (within the current year) and any bills that are being disputed. Keep the following vital documents, and any others you might have, in a safety deposit box:

- Birth and death certificates.
- Adoption papers.
- Marriage license.
- Divorce decree.
- Deeds to any and all property.
- Car titles.
- Bills for all major household purchases—furniture, jewelry, electronics, appliances.
- Power of Attorney.

Do not put your original will in your safety deposit box. Let your attorney hold your original, and you keep a copy at home.

Remember that you are in control of what you read. These days, we're bombarded with letters, brochures, pamphlets, fliers, and other documents. It's remarkable how much detailed information the power company sends us to read with our bills each month—some even send monthly newsletters—as though we're that fascinated about where our electricity's coming from! If you're living in the 21st century, it's a given that far more printed matter will pass through your hands than you can possibly read and process, let alone file. Just because they send it doesn't mean you have to read it—or keep it.

a note from
the instructor

KEEP YOUR NAME OFF JUNK-MAILERS' LISTS, E-MAIL LISTS, AND PHONE LISTS

■ Don't send in warranty cards for products you buy unless you need to be informed of recalls (which are particularly important with baby items).

■ Don't fill out sweepstakes entries.

■ Don't put your e-mail address on any Web site registration forms.

■ Register a temporary address change rather than a permanent one with the Postal Service. They sell their permanent list but not their temporary address changes.

One additional word about paper management: You must maintain your systems. I recommend that you purge your reference files once or twice a year.

How to Handle Mail

I advocate sorting incoming mail on a daily basis. The first phase requires only that you do a quick sort to get rid of all the junk mail. If you stand over a wastebasket when you do this, you'll get rid of at least half of your incoming mail. Place the remaining mail in an inbox to be processed at a designated time. I've found that scheduling time once a week works well for most people.

BOOKS AND MAGAZINES

Many of us hoard books out of a misplaced sense of reverence. Throwing away a battered book seems almost as sacrilegious as tossing away a tattered flag. If you're not likely to read it again, though, it's not doing you any good. Let it go to make way for new books.

If you have hardbacks in decent condition, on subjects that don't become outdated too quickly, you might be able to get good money for them online or through a yard sale. You could also donate them to your favorite library, school, or charity. Book swaps with friends are good, too.

Paperbacks are a different story. They're made cheaply, designed to be read once or twice, and then meant to be thrown away. They're worth very little used and practically nothing if they're chipped, torn, stained, or have cracked spines. Once they get that way, they're an eyesore and difficult to read. The odds of you picking them up again grow smaller and smaller, and they degenerate further and further into clutter.

Replace your favorite books with hardbound copies in better condition, and then treat them as a collection and display them. Designate one wall in your home for bookcases. Turn a closet into a library by removing its door, filling it with bookshelves, and lighting it.

Nearly everyone owns at least some books, yet we seldom remember to design a place for them in our household plans. Books are beautiful, and they're a reflection of you and your interests. They deserve to be treated with respect. You'll also like the effect they'll have on your kids if you give them a prominent place of honor in your home.

Magazines are also an enormous trouble spot for many of us. We often don't even know how many magazine subscriptions we have. My students complain that they seldom have time to read the magazines they get, but since they keep arriving each month, the magazines keep accumulating. It's an understandable impulse: We paid good money for them, so we can't just throw them away! But again, if you're not reading them, then they're not serving you.

Cancel any subscriptions to magazines that you haven't read in the last six months. For those magazines that you choose to keep, peruse each issue as it arrives and mark the articles you genuinely want to read. Forget the rest. Read what's of interest, and then pass them along to a friend, give them to a doctor's office, or toss them out.

"Toss them *all* out?" you ask, with horror in your voice. "Even *Smithsonian*...and *National Geographic?*" If you have children who will use high-end magazines like this for reference, I won't try to talk you out of keeping them, but let me make one last appeal about magazines, particularly the high-quality ones: Your local library probably has them all. Why not visit the library when you need to look at a particular issue, and let *them* take care of the storage?

a note from
the instructor

CASH IN YOUR USED BOOKS

The used books that bring the best returns from a used bookstore, yard sale, or online auction (like Half.com, Amazon.com, and HalfPriceBooks.com) are quality hardcovers in near-perfect condition that are written on highly marketable subjects that stand the test of time. Best-sellers and quality art books generally age well; travel books and textbooks go out of style quickly.

With hardcover books, it's the jacket that makes the all-important first impression. The book's value plummets if the jacket isn't in excellent condition. You'll get more for a book with a glossy jacket that has no corners missing. If you're going to resell a book, don't write in it— not even your name—unless, of course, you're the author.

MUSIC AND MOVIES

I once organized the home of the president of a recording company. He owned more than 6,000 CDs! He had an excuse—his profession. But many of us just don't seem to know where to stop when it comes to CDs, DVDs, and videos.

I mean that literally. We don't know where to stop because we've never set a limit for ourselves. Unless music or film is your profession, there's a limit to the number of recordings that you'll actually be able to keep track of. I advise students to set their personal limit and stick to it. When you've reached your limit, get rid of some CDs before you buy more.

Organize your collection by type of music or film (jazz, blues, rock, classical, and so forth for music; drama, western, science fiction, comedy, romance, and so on for films). Alphabetize within categories. Then, when you have a yen to buy new ones, peruse your collection for items you no longer watch or listen to.

Have you tried swapping CDs with friends? I've recommended this to my students, and it seems to be an enormous success. I like this because it not only keeps your collection from stagnating and becoming clutter, it also adds a new social dimension to its use.

TOYS AND GAMES

How many times have you heard someone from an older generation express astonishment at the number of toys our kids own today? Our culture offers children a never-ending array of gift-giving occasions. Unfortunately, many busy parents and grandparents these days find it easier to appease with toys than to spend time with their children or grandchildren. Add the fact that we seldom take the time to sort through our children's possessions and teach them the fine art of weeding out the broken and unused, and you have the perfect recipe for a nation of stuffed closets and jam-packed toy chests.

We know it's just a matter of time before the next birthday party, Happy Meal, or grandparents' visit. No matter how fast we get rid of the toys, new ones are already on the way.

There's no labor-free solution to this problem. We have to help our kids grow to be the responsible, organized, clutter-free people that we aim to be. If we want room for new toys when they come, we have to let go of some of the old ones first.

 a note from
the instructor

NIX THE TOY BOX

Do your children keep most of their toys in a single huge toy box? If your answer is yes, I almost don't need to ask the next question. Is their toy box an unqualified disaster area? Odds are that your kids can't find the toy they're looking for buried among all that clutter. If they do find it, it will probably be broken from the jumble of other toys heaped on top of it.

Gather your kids together and sort through all their toys in the same way I've outlined sorting through adult possessions. Once you're left with the keepers, you'll be able to assess what kind of toy storage would actually serve their play and maximize their enjoyment of their toys.

Consider open shelves for attractive toys, small plastic shoeboxes (labeled) for action figures, cars, small plastic animals, magnetic letters, and the like.

And by the way, don't throw out that empty toy box. I promise you'll find it useful for storing something else!

a note from
the instructor

TURNING CLUTTER INTO COLLECTIONS

Do you collect baseball cards? Marbles? Matchbooks? Whatever your particular passion, does your collection live in a musty box under your bed or in a handsome display for all to see?

You'll get even more enjoyment out of whatever you collect if your storage is also a display unit. Most small items (arrowheads, coins, miniatures) do beautifully in museum-style glass cases, whether wall-mounted or tabletop. Other items (ball caps, etc.) look best hanging from hooks on the wall. Still others (record albums and other "flat" items) are displayed to their greatest advantage in frames.

Whatever method you choose, putting your collection on display is the best way to assure that it remains a collection and doesn't degenerate into mere clutter.

Unless it's a special toy, an antique, or extremely expensive, encourage your child to throw it out when it's broken, and give it away or sell it when it's no longer used. Exercise discretion about what toys come into your home in the first place. Don't even get fast-food meals with toys (they're usually uninspired toys anyway), unless you keep them in a special lidded bin.

There's no law that says you have to keep a toy for a certain length of time. Kids are most fascinated with toys when they're brand new and still a novelty. If a toy doesn't look like a keeper (if it's playability is limited, if it doesn't offer much educational value, or if it's poorly made), how about letting your kids enjoy it for a few days and then letting it go? You could even set up a special bin for "temporary toys," destined to be used for a short time then launched back into the Great Cosmic Toy Bin.

If your kids have outgrown a toy, give it away. It's fine to keep one small bin or basket of "little-kid toys" for your guests' children; make sure the bin can be tucked away out of sight when the kids go home. Put a sensible limit—and a lid—on what you do keep.

Everything I've said about toys also applies to games, with the added complication that nearly every game has lots of tiny parts that just love to find their way all over the house. Anticipate this in advance. Bag small parts; wrap a rubber band around cards. If your kids are below the age of six, supervise them when they take out games with lots of small pieces. Make a fun ritual of rounding up all the pieces when the game is finished. If a game is missing parts and you don't know where to call for replacements, get rid of it. Likewise with puzzles.

HOW TO HANDLE CHILDREN'S ARTWORK

Make sure that every type of treasure you collect has a place and a plan. If your kids are always drawing sweet little pictures with "I love you" scribbled across the top, and you can't bear to throw them out, keep a container for each child's drawings, where you can put them once they've been displayed lovingly on the fridge. Each child should have their own container for keepsakes, and I suggest that you go through it with your child at the end of the school year and decide on a handful of favorites. Mark the date and year on them.

HOW TO HANDLE HOBBIES AND COLLECTIONS

If you collect recipes, give them a box or scrapbook to live in. If you collect fliers for events, consider a 12-month accordion file. Know your collections: Arrange your space to accommodate them, create a plan for dealing with them, and schedule time to do so.

PHOTOS

When I ask my students what one thing they would save if they ever had to evacuate their homes, without exception all of them answer, "My photographs." But in my experience people don't dedicate the time to keeping and enjoying their most prized possessions.

I suspect that photos are prone to becoming clutter because we store them away for some anonymous later moment when we'll have time to organize them. "I just figured I'd make the memories now, and then I could sort out the pictures when my kids are grown up and I have time on my hands," a student once told me. However, if your pictures aren't stored properly, when the time finally comes to organize your memories, you may discover that your precious, irreplaceable photos haven't survived intact and that you no longer remember who's doing what where and when.

Do yourself a favor and store your photos for the long haul from the beginning. First, designate an area for the project. If you have the luxury of space, pick an area you can leave undisturbed because the project will probably take a long period of time. Wear 100% cotton gloves when you handle photos. Gather all your photos and sort them chronologically, first by decade, then by year. You can also sort them by event if you wish (weddings, bar mitzvahs, etc.). Cull the blurry, dark, and unflattering ones. Throw them away. Why do we have such an aversion to tossing photos in the trashcan? If they're lousy or incomprehensible, they're clutter. If you made too many duplicates, send them to a relative.

Mark each photo on the back with as much information as you can, using a pencil designed especially for marking photos. Follow the same system with your negatives (but don't write on them). Then store the organized photos and negatives in an archival-quality photo container. You can then easily go through them and pull out your favorites whenever you're ready to place them in albums or in frames. Don't hang photos in direct sunlight. Never laminate them. Don't keep your photos in a basement, attic, garage, or anyplace that extreme temperatures and dampness can affect them.

student experience

"My grandmother was the family genealogist. Every time we saw her, she told us stories about our relatives. She also saved every photograph, legal document, and newspaper clipping that featured one of our family members. When she died at the age of 97, the task of sorting through all these photos and documents fell on her youngest son, my father. He had inherited her love of family history, and he knew what these mementos meant to my grandmother, but he had a very difficult time sorting through the 14 shoeboxes of photographs. Many of the photographs had no writing on the back to identify the people in them, and, as he said, 'How many pictures of your Great Uncle Orlando do we really need?'

"My grandmother's collection was full of treasures, but it took my father months to sort through everything and make the painful decision of whether to keep or throw away each item."

—Tim, editor

a note from
the instructor

PHOTO STORAGE DOS AND DON'TS

Don't:

- Store pictures in envelopes or cardboard shoeboxes—the acid and lignin in the paper causes the photos to become brittle and discolored.
- Use magnetic photo albums—the acidity can destroy the photo over time.
- Keep your pictures in a basement, attic, or anywhere that temperature and moisture can go through severe changes.

Do:

- Throw away dark, out of focus, or unflattering photos.
- Organize your photos by category: people, events, etc., and then organize each category chronologically.
- Buy archival-quality albums.
- Write dates, places, people, and other notes on the back with a special photo pencil.

DONATING, RECYCLING, AND DUMPING

Now that you've culled the keepers from the clutter in each category, how do you decide what to do with the stuff you no longer want? I'll assume that you're civically minded and environmentally conscious, and that your first choice would be to donate the item to someone in need, or to recycle it if possible, leaving the county landfill as the last choice. Let's look at each of these in turn.

- **Donating:** By all means, donate your unwanted stuff to your favorite charity, school, church, or synagogue. Sometimes you may have to do a little work to find the right recipient, but it's worth at least a little effort. If you succeed, get a receipt for your taxes. Make sure that everything you donate is in good condition.

- **Recycling:** Some metal scrap yards will take used appliances for free—call ahead to make sure. Also bring in your used newspapers, cans, glass, bulk metals, and certain plastics.

Don't do this expecting to come away with a hefty chunk of cash; the odds are that what you'll get for your recyclables, if anything, won't even buy you an ice cream cone. Your real reward comes from knowing that your clutter won't be taking up space in a landfill.

■ **Dumping:** Strange as it may seem, even throwing away your unwanted possessions will cost you money. Once you've spent the time and money to get rid of them, though, they won't cost you any more in the future. Most dumps charge by the pound, and may charge you extra to dispose of tires, appliances, some chemicals, and "construction debris." Remember to identify and dispose of harzardous materials properly (for instance, house paint, batteries, household cleaners, automobile oil and fluids, and the like).

Not all dumps accept every type of junk. Some only take clean dirt, some only yard refuse, and so forth. Some will not take tires or appliances. Call the dump before you load up your car with junk and head out there.

Drive to the top of a well-stuffed landfill on a hot day, and you'll never receive a more sobering lesson in the impact of our obsession with things on the world at large. You're standing on a veritable *mountain* of clutter.

It's not fun to have to resort to the landfill to get rid of your unwanted items—if you're environmentally conscious at all, you'll feel it. Use that uncomfortable sensation as an incentive to curb your tendency to accumulate extra stuff.

YARD SALES, CLASSIFIED ADS, AND ONLINE AUCTIONS

Make sure you measure the cost of yard sales versus donating—both in terms of time and money. You may get a lot more for your stuff as a tax write-off than you will from selling it. Don't waste a lot of time on yard sales unless you live in a neighborhood that's conducive to them. If your home is in a poor yard-sale location, you might opt for a community yard sale at a local church, recreation center, or flea market. Price things to move—people shop at yard sales for bargains, not treasures.

For larger-ticket items (barbecue grills, computers, etc.), take out an ad in your local cheapie classified publication—nearly every town has one. They're often called something like *Penny Pincher*.

Putting an object up for online auction (for instance, on Ebay.com or Half.com) works well if the item is attractive, desirable, popular, or rare, and will ship cheaply and safely. It should be in nearly pristine condition, and you must note any flaws, even minor ones, in your ad. Make the opening bid tantalizingly low or you risk attracting no bidders. Describe the item as clearly as you can in your auction's title line—think about what phrases potential bidders might be using as they search for such an item. If you can get a picture in with your auction, you'll substantially increase the number of visitors to your site. For more information, consult a specialty book such as *eBay for Dummies, 4th Edition*.

Now, a word of caution. After you've put your items up for auction, resist the temptation to visit other auctions and load up on other people's stuff. How many people do you know who have sold more than they've bought online?

UNCLUTTERING LESSON-END QUESTIONS

Lesson #5:

1. List the documents that are most important to you: the ones you know you'll need in the future and that would be difficult to replace.

_____

_____

_____

2. Now list several types of documents you routinely keep that *don't* belong on the list above. How many of these documents could you safely do without?

_____

_____

_____

3. List all your magazine, newspaper, and newsletter subscriptions. Place an X next to the ones you'd be willing to do without. Place an E next to the ones you could access online instead of receiving in paper form. Place an L next to the ones your local library carries. Cancel the ones with an X or L. Switch your subscription to the online version for the ones with an E.

_____

_____

_____

4. What objects are you currently storing that could bring you more joy if they were on display?

_____

_____

_____

Other Thoughts:

_____

_____

_____

_____

_____

_____

redesign your environment to prevent clutter

Sanitize • Minimize • Containerize • Compartmentalize

Once you've defined your goals for arranging your home and workspace, and have pared down your possessions to those that are actively serving you, you're ready to make sure that each item you own has a place to live when it's not in use. If the setup of your home is conducive to organization, this task is much easier. Regardless of size, age, value, or style, you can make any home more "organization friendly" by the way you furnish and maintain it.

Houses that are kept clean and dust-free stand a better chance of fending off clutter. Similarly, rooms that have most objects stowed conveniently out of sight—except those that have aesthetic value or are in near-constant use—can contain an enormous number of possessions but never look cluttered. Objects that you keep in a logical order (in labeled containers, for instance), stand a better chance of winding up back where they're supposed to be.

The following four rules will help you organize the appearance and functionality of a room and help keep clutter in check: sanitize, minimize, containerize, and compartmentalize. Let's take a closer look at each one.

SANITIZE

Cleanliness is a natural clutter repellent. Mice, ants, and even teenagers are less likely to mess with an area that looks pristine and orderly. Cleanliness sends a message of purpose. It also has a way of

 a note from
the instructor

EIGHT WAYS TO REDUCE CLEANING TIME

1. Organize cleaning supplies and tools; store them in a bin with a handle or on a rolling cart so they're ready to travel with you to each room. Cleaning materials that are well organized and easy to access are also much more likely to be used.

2. Set brushy, dirt-trapping mats before each exterior door and at the top of basement steps to head off the *schmutz* that might otherwise get tracked into the living areas of your home.

3. If your environment gets dusty quickly, consider investing in an air purifier to filter out some of the pollutants you'd otherwise have to wipe up.

4. If you have very small children, consider painting walls below chair rail height (3.5 feet) with gloss or semi-gloss, or covering them with some other type of easy-wipe surface.

5. If you cook frequently on your range top, make sure your hood and blower are in good working order and that they vent outside. Run the fan anytime you cook on the range top. Grease combined with dust makes for one of the most time-consuming cleanups. Remember to periodically clean the filters in your hood to keep them working properly.

6. If your house has many horizontal blinds on the windows, invest in a slatted horizontal blind cleaner that makes quick work of this normally time-consuming chore.

7. Clean frequently for short periods, when things are "slightly dirty," so that you never have to spend hours scrubbing a disaster area.

8. Have family members do a quick wipe-down of the tub or shower after each use, or try misting with a daily shower cleaning spray.

elevating your mood; it's easier to maintain a positive outlook when everything's spiffy and sparkling-clean.

Keep your possessions—both seen and unseen—clean and dust-free. Wherever possible, head off the dirt before it settles on your possessions. If you live in a dusty area, consider investing in an air purifier to help remove dust, pollen, dander, and other pollutants from the air before it gets on your things.

If family members track mud, leaves, and grass into the house, place doormats strategically at entryways. If fast-food wrappers and soda cans tend to collect in a particular area, sneak a trashcan into the spot and encourage people to use it. If your spouse drops socks by the side of the bed every night, plop a laundry basket right where they land. If your spouse complains of tripping over the basket in the middle of the night, smile lovingly and praise his or her sacrifice on behalf of your organizing efforts.

Stay ahead of the dirt. Never let it accumulate. Build a small amount of cleaning time into your daily and weekly schedule, and cleaning will never become the unwieldy time-gobbler that's capable of devouring an entire weekend.

MINIMIZE

As a rule, the more physical objects you can see in a room, the more chaotic and disorganized it appears. A room can hold an enormous number of objects and still look tidy as long as most of what's there is concealed, and if what does meet the eye is nicely arranged.

Cabinets, closets, and drawers aren't the only ways to make items vanish. Cubbies and cubes with curtained fronts or with baskets that slide in and out work wonders for multiple items like shoes or school supplies. These type of baskets are currently very popular, so they are easy to find. They're also a great way to make better use of vertical space. They help you organize in terms of *cubic* feet instead of square feet. Decorative boxes, attractive covered baskets, trunks, and furniture with built-in storage can also be used to keep objects out of sight. If you have open shelving, consider covering it with curtains or vertical blinds.

Ultimately, it has less to do with the number of items you own and everything to do with what's in plain sight. If it's ugly or utilitarian, get it out of sight. If it's pretty or intriguing, set it up on display.

You can still arrange an item in a way that's functional, even if it's also décor. Many sewing stores now sell thread organizers designed to hold several rows of spools on spindles set at an angle. These holders allow you to locate the thread you want quickly and pull out the length you need without ever having to handle the spool, but it also allows your colorful, shiny thread to brighten the room with its homey, decorative presence.

The real difference between clutter and austerity is not just a matter of how few items you display; it also matters how many items appear to be where they should be.

When evaluating possible storage areas, think creatively. Don't limit yourself to the obvious solutions. Kitchen cabinets are intended to store food and food-related items, but if you're lucky enough to have extra storage in your kitchen, you have almost unlimited storage possibilities. These cabinets can house children's arts and crafts supplies. They also make perfect places to store your toolbox, sewing box, and first aid kit (it's important that your whole family know where the first aid kit is located).

A student once complained that she had insufficient storage for her rather large shoe collection. The single closet in her bedroom was small,

---

 a note from
the instructor

HIDE OR DISPLAY?

Hide it if it's:

- Ugly.
- Awkward.
- Utilitarian.
- Made up of many little pieces.

Arrange the rest harmoniously:

- Treat whatever remains unstowed as a display.
- Arrange it aesthetically with attractive spacing between objects.
- Where appropriate, light it to signify that it's on display.
- Group like items together.

and she had to share what little hanging space she had with her husband. Her shoes were piled on the floor of the closet and were beginning to encroach on the hanging garments. The closet had accordion-style doors that provided no storage solution, and the bedroom was too small to consider replacing those doors with anything that would accommodate storage. In thinking about alternative solutions, we discovered that she had a long, built-in wall unit in the hall right outside of the bedroom. While the top of the unit was full of books on open shelves, there was *nothing* stored in the cabinets beneath. Now those cabinets are filled with shoes—all neatly placed and organized by season, color, and style. This single change has shaved 15 minutes from the amount of time it takes my student to get ready for work each morning.

CONTAINERIZE

Unless they're very large, most objects destined for storage will need more than just a shelf or cabinet. Photos, memorabilia, hobby materials, and anything with small parts, irregular pieces, or graded sizes will need to be contained or they'll continue to be clutter. This is where baskets, boxes, and bins become a necessity—I'll discuss these in depth in the next lesson, but for now let's work on the principle behind them.

Most of your possessions will need to have some kind of boundary ascribed to them—even items that stand in plain view have a defined space where they belong. The bill organizer lives on the shelf right above your workstation, *not* on the filing cabinet across the room that you would have to get up and walk over to every time you needed to reference a bill.

If the container itself will show, give some thought to its appearance. Just because it's a storage container doesn't mean it must look utilitarian. Attractive organizing is so popular today that you'll find entire stores devoted to "pretty" bins, boxes, baskets, and whatnot. When selecting a container, keep function foremost in your mind; sensible storage is your best defense against clutter.

Label all containers clearly. If nobody can read your handwriting on a label—including you—then no one will use the containers, and you will have wasted your time. I'm an advocate of label-printing machines; they'll more than pay for themselves with the amount of frustration they'll save you. You can also set up your computer to print labels. Any office supply store sells sheets of labels designed for use with a printer.

a note from the instructor

ITEMS TO LABEL

In the kitchen:

- Shelves.
- Drawers.
- Spices.
- Jars of food.
- Freezer packages (with date).
- Leftovers (with date).

In the garden:

- Fertilizers.
- Insecticides.
- Plant stakes.
- Plant tags.
- Seed packets.
- Hoses (mark length).
- Garden tool pegboards (mark where each tool goes).

Around the house:

- Breaker switches on fuse box.
- Smoke detectors (date of last battery change).

In the workshop and garage:

- Paint cans.
- Small hardware bins.
- Pegboards (name the item that goes in each place).

At the office:

- File drawers.
- File folders.
- Binders.
- Computer disks.
- Shelves.
- Trays.
- Organizer pockets.
- Computer/electrical cables.

I'm not trying to disparage your handwriting; if your printing is very neat and you *prefer* writing your labels by hand, then by all means you should do it that way. Just be consistent—visual uniformity is more calming.

If you need to switch labels often on a particular set of containers, use cardboard or wooden boxes and paint the fronts with chalkboard paint. Then use chalk to list the boxes' contents right on the front of the box. You can also use boxes made of smooth melamine (or glue a lightweight sheet of melamine to the front), and you've got an instant dry-erase labeling surface.

In general, use the same size and type of container for all the items in a particular collection. For instance, by keeping all your DVDs in the same-size boxes, your collection will look much neater, and because the whole grouping will be easier on the eye, it will take less time to zero in on the disc you're after.

When you know you're about to do a lot of organizing, it's tempting to rush out and buy an armload of different-sized containers and a bunch of those wonderful little plastic drawer organizers. But be careful. Too many organizing tools can themselves become a form of clutter. I'd recommend instead that you organize your items first, decide what kind of organizing system will work best, determine what you already

a note from
the instructor

TWICE AS USEFUL: FURNITURE
WITH BUILT-IN STORAGE

The next time you shop for furniture, choose multifunctional pieces that include built-in storage. You'll find a number of options at every price level and to complement every décor. Check local furniture stores for these ingenious items:

- Captain's bed with built-in storage underneath.
- Coffee table with magazine storage built in.
- Unit that doubles as a bed and a table.
- Ottoman that opens to provide space for storage.
- Bench with a storage compartment.
- Stool with a storage compartment.

have that you can use, and then make a list of exactly what your system still requires. This way, you'll only buy what you truly need—the ultimate secret to avoiding clutter!

COMPARTMENTALIZE

This is where your "macro" and "micro" planning for each room really come into play. In any given room, you'll have areas designated for particular activities or particular types of items. Make sure every item has its designated area, whether shelf, drawer, bin, or other storage. Then, within that area, assign each item its specific place.

For instance, your garlic press belongs in the food-preparation area of your kitchen; that's its "macro" destination. Within the food preparation area, it's grouped with small utensils used infrequently (unless you *really* love garlic). So it will probably go in the "small, infrequently used utensils" drawer, along with your knife sharpener and egg slicer.

Unless, that is, your garlic press is very special. If it's an antique heirloom from Italy, with hand-painted porcelain handles and brass plating, don't you dare toss it in a drawer! Why not arrange it in a basket with a couple of beautiful, papery-white garlic cloves and an attractive bottle of olive oil—maybe even alongside a potted basil plant?

On the other extreme, suppose you hate garlic and you never cook with it. So why in the world are you hanging onto a garlic press in the first place? Get that blasphemy out of your kitchen!

 a note from the instructor

RULES FOR STORAGE

- Think cubic feet not square feet. When you're planning storage, think about the height and depth of each area, not just floor space and shelf space.
- Utilize vertical space.
- Think outside the box.
- Be creative.

The more frequently an item is needed, the more accessible it should be. If it's needed infrequently but you have to have it in a hurry when it's needed (like first aid supplies), then you don't need to have it right at your elbow. Save that precious space for items you use several times each day. Still, you will want to keep even an infrequently used item within easy reach and clearly visible so that you don't have to move other items to get to it.

UNCLUTTERING LESSON-END QUESTIONS

Lesson #6:

1. List some of the steps you could take to head off the accumulation of clutter and dirt around your home.

_____

_____

_____

2. List some of the things you could do to streamline and organize the way you clean your home.

_____

_____

_____

3. What areas of your home get dirty and disorganized the quickest?

_____

_____

_____

4. What could you do to keep these areas under control?

_____

_____

_____

5. In each room, look at the items that are sitting out. Which of these items could be stored out of sight until you need them? List them here, and then list possible storage places for each item.

_____

_____

_____

bins, drawers, cabinets, shelves, and beyond

Determining Types of Storage • Bins • Boxes • Baskets • Cabinets • Drawers • Shelves • Closets • Unconventional Storage

In this lesson we'll take a closer look at the storage options available to you and help you make an informed decision about what type of storage is best for the "micro" portion of your planning.

Creativity is the watchword here. Think outside the box. Feel free to come up with storage ideas that nobody's ever thought of before. Paint colorful designs of your own making on plain wooden crates, wallpaper a series of plastic buckets with your doodles, paste pictures of your favorite animals on your file boxes—make your containers your own. If you can create a storage system that meets your need for functionality but also serves as a form of self-expression, you've got something that serves you twice. The more attractive and fun you can make it, the more likely you'll be to use it faithfully.

Also think beyond your inclination to rush out to the nearest container store and plunk down a week's salary on some shiny new set of organizers. The world is full of fabulous (and often fabulously expensive) organizing products. You're welcome to buy them if you truly want them. But you can also satisfy some of your organizing needs with cheap, free, built-from-scratch, and recycled storage devices. Use what you have before you buy something new.

student experience

"Labeling was the secret for me. I found that I needed large storage bins to hold all of my seasonal decoration, but I hated having to crack each one open to find the one I needed. I finally took my digital camera, snapped pictures of some of my favorite items from each box, and then turned the pictures into labels. Now identifying the boxes is a cinch."

—Mike, public relations

Have a baby, or know someone who does? Collect those baby food jars—they're terrific for holding small hardware in the workshop and tiny parts from any craft or hobby. Save the plastic tube-shaped containers that powdered drink mixes come in, soak off the labels, and you've got a neat, trim series of canisters for crayons, embroidery floss, or what-have-you. Ice cube trays are great for storing earrings.

As you're deciding on the right type of container for each area, consider the strengths and weaknesses of the options available. Baskets, might look cozy and rustic, but they're bulky, so they might not be suitable for tight spaces. Cardboard file boxes are cheap and flexible, but if you've got bunches of them lining your office walls, your clients may find them less than attractive. Even worse, they may get the impression that your business is unstable, or that you're always moving from place to place.

The following sections of this lesson take a closer look at your storage options.

STORAGE BY FUNCTION

Different types and groupings of objects require different types of storage, depending on their function and on the frequency of their use. To get the most out of your organizing systems, choose the right kind of storage for each given item. The following tables offer a quick overview of some creative options.

FLAT ITEMS

STORAGE DEVICE	ITEMS STORED
Typesetting trays with compartments removed	Art paper, flatware

FRAGILE ITEMS

STORAGE DEVICE	ITEMS STORED
Used light bulb boxes	Breakable holiday ornaments
Muffin tin	Miniatures
Poster Mailer	Swags, garlands, posters
Wooden crate	Large, heavy breakables (vases, statues)

ITEMS WITH MANY PARTS

STORAGE DEVICE	ITEMS STORED
Coffee cans	Kids' craft supplies, extra hardware, extra cords, extra baby-proofing supplies
Drink mix containers	Pencils, pens, art supplies
Shoeboxes	Paper, cards, art supplies, correspondence
Typesetting tray	Beads and other small hobby supplies

LARGE BULKY OBJECTS

STORAGE DEVICE	ITEMS STORED
Large plastic bins	Wreaths, large decorative items, party supplies, seasonal linens
File cabinet	Sweaters, blankets, pots and pans
Garbage bags	Seasonal linens, spare pillows (use a vacuum to remove air and seal with a rubber band)
Large suitcases	Other luggage and bags
Computer paper box	Stuffed animals, toys
Plastic crates	Stuffed animals, toys
Shoeboxes	Small toys by type

LARGE UGLY ITEMS

STORAGE DEVICE	ITEMS STORED
Screen	Exercise equipment
Curtain	Washer/dryer, vacuum, cubbies

LONG ITEMS

STORAGE DEVICE	ITEMS STORED
Wall hooks	Poles, long-handled tools
Canvas/nylon straps slung from ceiling beams	Skis

ODDLY SHAPED ITEMS

STORAGE DEVICE	ITEMS STORED
Crates	Toys, small appliances, craft supplies
Baskets	Magazines, remote controls, condiments
Plastic storage containers	Toys, seasonal items
Tins	Cooking implements, office supplies
Canisters	Cooking implements

PAPERS

STORAGE DEVICE	ITEMS STORED
Shoeboxes	Correspondence, cards
Hanging file box	One for old records, labeled and in storage, one for current year's records only, put in storage after the year's taxes are done, start a new one each January
Archive box	Last five to seven years of financial records
Computer paper boxes	Select pieces of kids' artwork, last five to seven years of financial records

SEMI-PERISHABLE FOODS

STORAGE DEVICE	ITEMS STORED
Glass jars	Rice, pasta, flour, mixes
Cookie tins	Bags of herbs and spices

SHARP ITEMS

STORAGE DEVICE	ITEMS STORED
Block of florist's foam	Awls and craft blades (stick in block)
Soap or wax	Pins, needles

SMALL ITEMS

STORAGE DEVICE	ITEMS STORED
Ice cube trays	Earrings, jewelry, craft items
Egg cartons	Earrings, craft items, jewelry
Baby food jars	Hardware, small craft items
Drawer divider or subdivided open top container	Hosiery, hair accessories, jewelry, makeup, rolled socks

STRINGY ITEMS

STORAGE DEVICE	ITEMS STORED
Plastic soda bottles (cut in half—feed string through bottleneck and store inside)	Yarn, twine
Dowels mounted on board	Spools

Compartmentalized Organization

Documents, photos, and collections of similar items that need to be sorted in a utilitarian manner should be stored in a number of compartments arranged in a particular order. Photos (as we discussed in a previous lesson) should be organized chronologically by subject. The containers you choose for photo storage must serve this type of organization. You should be able to label them clearly with the subject and date of the photos they contain, and you should be able to easily reference the photos you're looking for so that you can get them back to their proper places with a minimum of effort.

Think in terms of bill organizers, accordion files, and wall pockets—imagine other ways they might be useful. For small- to medium-sized items, choose a series of matching containers that are all the same size and label them. For items too large to go inside a container, label their places on the shelf or tabletop.

Safekeeping

Items that need to be protected for the long term require storage that provides maximum protection. The type of protection depends on the item and the storage area. Wrap any fabrics or papers in archival-grade polyester film or plain prewashed muslin. Store them in archival-quality boxes in a *dry* location. Fold fine linen as little as possible. Don't mix different types of collections—their materials may not be compatible, and one could cause the other to degrade. For instance, plastics release gases that can destroy paper—a plastic bumper sticker could ruin a paper letter. Unfold letters and put acid-free tissue between each page.

Items stored for safekeeping are, by nature, not the sort of things you'll need every day, so they should be packed to withstand being tucked away in their containers for long periods of time. Place moth repellents in with garments, and protect paper and fabric from moisture and light. Wrap breakables carefully in foam or bubble wrap.

If you have a wine collection, or want to preserve those fine cigars, be sure you store them properly so that they'll be in peak condition when you decide to enjoy them. This is the time to seek the advice of experts for storage suggestions. Specialty magazines or specialty stores will often be your best sources for locating appropriate storage advice.

Concealment

Unsightly items—such as vacuum cleaners, bathroom cleansers, and dirty clothes—should always be hidden from view. Aside from closet doors, think in terms of curtains, Venetian blinds, and pocket doors.

Display

You may want to make some attractive and interesting items part of your home's décor. Heirloom tableware and collections of all kinds fit into this category. Your choices here depend on the nature of the collection—should it hang from the wall, sit atop a table, or stand on a shelf?

If your collection is made up of flat items, you have a dazzling array of framing options at your disposal. Many companies now make frames sized to fit LPs or to display sports jerseys. These frames are pricey, though, and you can get almost as nice an effect by framing your jerseys in a poster frame for a fraction of the cost. If you must keep your Beanie Baby collection, consider storing them in a multipocket hanging shoe bag. Sports caps look pretty cool hanging from wall hooks set in even rows.

For bulkier items, or fragile ones, consider glass-fronted display cases. These too can be pricey, but there's no rule that says you can't build your own from leftover lumber and then drop in glass from frames you picked up at a yard sale for 25 cents apiece.

a note from
the instructor

STORAGE LEVELS

■ Frequently used items—between waist and eye level
■ Secondary or heavy items—below waist
■ Infrequently used items—space above eye level

Once you have your collection nicely displayed, consider making it even more of an attention-grabber by lighting it attractively. Spotlighting and track lighting add a dramatic flair to a room and draw the eye straight to the object in their beams.

Reorganizing

This last one is a temporary storage category. It gives you a place to put items that are out of place until you're ready to put them back where they go. I often recommend to students that they keep a bin handy in every room that they occupy frequently; the bin is used to collect items that don't belong there. During your daily 10-minute pickup, you can grab this bin and whisk these items back to their proper places.

BINS

Unless they're highly decorative, the bins themselves need to be stowed and concealed (once they're holding the contents they're organizing). Fortunately, many bins are designed to stack well and slide onto shelves easily.

The lidded plastic tote-type bin is perfect for any place where moisture, sunlight, or dirt is a factor; they also work for items in long-term storage. These bins last almost forever and are so close to indestructible that you can practically run a truck over them. Remember, though, that their lids don't always close as tightly as you might think. Moisture can seep in if the air is really humid, and determined mice can sometimes squeeze through gaps in the lids.

Bins that fit beneath your bed work beautifully to organize an otherwise unwieldy—or often ignored—storage area. Just make sure you purchase bins with practical lids. Bins with lids that hinge poorly in the middle are not ideal to use beneath beds. You can buy lifts to set under your bed legs to raise the bed and give you 9 to 11 inches of extra storage space. But remember, you'll also need to get a longer bed skirt! Also be sure to label all bins according to their contents.

Boxes

Only use cardboard or similar storage boxes for out-of-sight storage. They're not pleasant to look at, and they can look cluttered if they aren't uniform in size. Remember that these are not appropriate for food items or archival purposes as I've discussed above. They are, however, an inexpensive and recyclable storage option.

Baskets

I've always had something of a love-hate relationship with baskets. They may lend themselves to your décor, but they can also be so bulky and unwieldy that they're practically useless. The exception to this is the type of basket (often found at organizing stores) that's basically a wicker box with handles and is designed to sit on a shelf or slide into a cubby.

If you're trying to use overhead space, you may want to consider hanging a series of Easter-style baskets (the kind with a top handle) from hooks on the ceiling. Using them this way is both aesthetically interesting and functional.

Use baskets primarily for irregular-sized unbreakable items such as yarn. Hang a tag from the handle that identifies each basket's contents.

Cabinets

Cabinets can be functional for both containment and concealment, and they can be built-in or freestanding. The most useful cabinets reach from floor to ceiling; the most attractive ones are built to match your home's architecture. If you want to use a cabinet for display, remove its doors or replace solid doors with glass-paned ones.

Drawers

In general, I like shelves and cabinets better than drawers. Drawers are more expensive and harder to adjust, and if they're too deep they can be difficult to get into. Drawers, especially shallow ones, can work particularly well for flat items like jewelry and scarves. The handiest drawers are those that mix and match deep with shallow, small with large. You can make a low-cost "faux drawer" out of a box or basket by gluing two dowels to the bottom to act as "runners" when you're sliding it in and out of its storage area.

Shelves

Customizing is the key to effective shelf use. Add dowels, moldings, and other custom touches to make attractive shelving that fits your décor. Place shelves wherever you can—even over doors and windows in smaller homes. Install shallow shelves in tight spaces. Where possible, let the shelves extend from floor to ceiling. In general, groupings of three shelves are easiest on the eye. Don't overlook recessed shelves as space-savers—sneak them into unused niches, like nonfunctioning fireplaces or former laundry chutes. Use hardwoods for beauty; pine for a more casual look; glass for kitchens, bathrooms, and displays; and melamine, fiberboard, and pegboard only where they won't be seen.

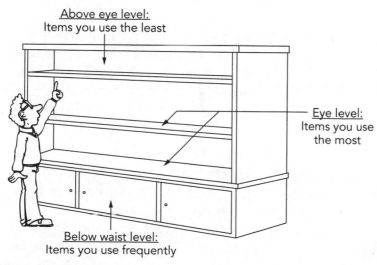

Above eye level:
Items you use the least

Eye level:
Items you use
the most

Below waist level:
Items you use frequently

Storage levels.

a note from
the instructor

ROOM DIVIDERS THAT OFFER STORAGE

- Armoires.
- Bookshelves set back-to-back.
- Decorative screens with pockets.

Be creative when it comes to storing items on your shelves. Not only do they work well for books and collections, but if you use your imagination and attractive containers, they can hold just about anything. I once had a student who worked as a stylist in the fashion industry. She lived in a small apartment in which she needed to store a multitude of accessories that she used in fashion shoots. To accommodate her needs, I suggested that she line two walls of her living room with shelves, buy wicker boxes with handles (described above), carefully label each and fill them with purses, scarves, and gloves. I also recommended that she hang a fabric curtain in front of the shelves to separate her home from her work and to add to the décor.

Closets

You absolutely must have a "micro" plan for each closet, or it will rapidly degenerate into a clutter pit. Fortunately, there is a vast array of closet-organizing products available for this purpose, as well as entire companies devoted to helping you get the most out of your closets. You can more than double the functional capacity of your closet by the way you arrange it.

Consider hanging a second closet rod 3 feet below the top one. If the closet primarily stores blouses, jackets, and pants (as opposed to long coats and dresses), you can hang twice as many items. Invest in high-quality hangers; the frustration they'll save you is more than worth the extra money you spend, plus your clothing will stay in shape longer. My favorites are clear plastic swivel hangers. Treat wire hangers as you would a highly contagious virus—banish them summarily from your home.

If space for pants and slacks is limited, consider installing a set of swinging pants rods on the inside of the closet door. This keeps a large number of pants in a very compact space and prevents them from vying for the same space as your shirts or blouses.

Sweaters, in general, shouldn't hang at all. They lose their shape and develop weird little indentations at the shoulders in the spot where the hangers dig in. Instead, fold sweaters and store them in boxes, bins, or drawers. Remember that any wardrobe item going into long-term storage should be dry-cleaned to remove any residual food stains that can attract mites and other nasty little critters. Don't store your clothes in dry-cleaning bags; chemicals in the plastic bags harm fabric over time.

Keep your wardrobe up-to-date and clutter-free with regular clearings. Toss any items you haven't worn in a year (with the exception of holiday and special-occasion items). If you're not sure about a particular item, hang it backward for a season. If it's still hanging that way at the end of the season, you're not using it enough to justify keeping it.

Once or twice a year you should set aside half a day and invite a friend over to help you go through your closet. Make sure it's an objective friend who's not afraid to tell you the truth. Then exchange the favor.

STORAGE IN UNLIKELY PLACES

Search vigorously for innovative storage locations. Hang things from the undersides of shelves in the kitchen (try hanging a paper towel holder or a wire rack for sponges and dishtowels). Store items on rolling carts that can carry what you need from room to room—or can vanish into a closet when they're not wanted.

Build a wine rack under a built-in table. Build storage cabinets around fireplaces. Build lidded window seats with storage bins under the cushions.

There's no limit to potential storage areas around your home, as long as you're willing to do some brainstorming.

a note from
the instructor

SNEAKY STORAGE: FIVE INGENIOUS PLACES TO STASH YOUR STUFF

Unused filing cabinet: Store bed linens, pots and pans, or bulky sweaters; if it locks, use it as a liquor cabinet.

Staircase landing: Install shallow (7- to 10-inch) bookshelves.

Spaces under staircases: Install shelving or a small desk, or transform it into a sewing corner.

Bay windows: Install window seats with hinged lids that conceal a storage compartment underneath.

Areas beneath hanging cabinets: Install hooks, pegs, loops, or tiny shelves.

UNCLUTTERING LESSON-END QUESTIONS

Lesson #7:

1. As you plan the storage for each room in your home, jot down ideas for containers. Consider not only what containers you could buy, but also think about what you have on hand that could be modified or decorated to suit your needs.

_____

_____

_____

2. For each room in your home, rank each storage area by accessibility: Is it best for items that are used every day, items used occasionally, or items used rarely? Refer to this list as you determine where your possessions should go.

_____

_____

_____

3. For each room, list any ideas you have for incorporating large storage units such as armoires, cubbies, and shelving.

_____

_____

_____

4. For each room, list unusual areas that might be turned into storage (for instance, the spaces over doorways).

_____

_____

_____

clutter-free kitchens

Pantries • Cooking Utensils • Tableware • Flatware • Kitchen Counters • Kitchen Cabinets • Refrigerators

Now that we've taken a closer look at some of the types of containers you might use in your "micro" areas, let's step back for a wider view and consider what's going on in the room as a whole. We'll start with that infamous clutter magnet, the kitchen. Remember that once you've pared down your belongings, your next step is to inventory everything you have in the kitchen and list everything you need so that you'll end up with the right storage units.

PANTRIES

Pantries can have the same magical potential as closets—they can be a tribute to efficiency or a black hole depending on the way they're arranged. Build in plenty of shelf space of varying heights: some for cans and jars, a few for tall bottles, along with some sturdy ones for bulk items. Finish your wooden pantry shelves with an easy-to-clean surface:

shelf paper, spar varnish, or high-gloss paint. You can also make your shelves out of plastic, melamine, or metal.

Store most pantry foods in airtight containers. Add a piece of the original package with the product name and cooking directions so you'll remember what it was and how to prepare it. If you're tight on space, consider using square containers that use space more economically than their round counterparts. Store potatoes, onions, squash, and garlic in baskets or bins for up to a month, but don't let onions touch potatoes—they'll spoil the potatoes.

student experience

"My mother once stored a case of taco shells on the shelf above an open container of powdered bathroom cleanser for several months. When she served the tacos, we all thought that they tasted like Ajax."
—Rhonda, veterinarian

Vinegar and most cooking oils can reside here too. However, rare or expensive vinegars and nut oils need to be refrigerated. Store bagged spices and seeds flat in a drawer or on a tray so they don't shift or spill. Store nonfood items elsewhere so they don't transfer flavors to your food. Anything with a strong chemical odor shouldn't be stored in your pantry at all.

If you're going to keep pet food in your pantry, store it on the pantry floor in a container of its own away from people food. Buy a container with a mouse-proof lid.

When you're planning your pantry, don't neglect to use the space on the back of the door (if it's a swinging door rather than a pocket door). Install hooks, shallow wire baskets, or hanging shoe pockets for additional storage.

Also make use of the pantry ceiling; screw in the kind of hooks made for hanging plants, and then hang a series of graduated wire baskets (which are great for storing potatoes and other hardy vegetables—they allow you to keep an eye on them and make sure they aren't sprouting), a mesh sack of unused cleaning rags, or a couple of smoked hams.

Schedule time about every three months to clear your pantry of old foods and other unused items. Be sure to wipe down the shelves when you do this.

COOKWARE

Many of us get into trouble when it comes to cookware. It gushes into our homes in the form of gifts, hand-me-downs, and impulse purchases ("Buy now, and we'll give you a second Omelet-Wiz *absolutely free!* But wait! There's more. . . ").

Open your utensil drawer and count the number of can openers you have. Three, four, more? How often will you actually need to open four cans simultaneously?

Pots and Pans

These are probably some of the bulkiest items your kitchen has to accommodate. If your kitchen has a relatively high ceiling, consider installing a rack with S-hooks from which you can hang pots and pans. I'd especially recommend doing this if a lot of your cookware is copper-bottomed, cast-iron, antique, pretty, or in some other fashion intriguing to look at. Hang these on a rack with S-hooks for easy access. If you don't have a tall-enough ceiling, mount a smaller rack on one wall.

If you do store your pots and pans in cabinets, nest and stack them to save space. Place a layer of felt or thin foam between each piece that you stack to keep them from sliding and scratching. Store their lids in graded sizes between vertical slats. If you have a large number of shallow frying pans or griddles, you may choose to store these vertically, too.

Stay on top of the condition of your pans, particularly those with nonstick coatings. A friend of mine used to hang on to old pans obsessively until there were huge, scratchy gray patches where the Teflon had completely chipped away. Her sister finally snuck into her kitchen and attached self-stick notes to each of the long-suffering pans. The notes read, "Please! Put me out of my misery!"

Once their surfaces start to go, replace them. It becomes increasingly difficult to cook with worn-out, nonstick pans. Make them last longer by cooking only with plastic or wooden utensils.

Utensils

If you have to wrench your utensil drawers open because they're so stuffed, you're not alone. Our aversion to throwing away kitchen gadgets is particularly strong, maybe because of the associations cooking gives us to home and comfort. It'd be like throwing away a part of mother!

But people are always giving us kitchen stuff. Remember what happened the first time you moved away from home into your very own apartment? Your mother, your aunts, and all their friends showed up with boxes of utensils to get you off to a good start. Their intentions were good, of course, but what they probably gave you was the stuff *they'd* been hoarding unused for decades. You probably ended up with drawers full of apple corers and shrimp de-veiners instead of a sensible set of kitchen basics. It snowballed from there. You collected gifts, yard sale items, and those infamous cookware sets that come with too many extras.

 a note from
the instructor

TRULY NECESSARY KITCHEN UTENSILS

In our consumption-driven society, we're forever tempted to buy fancy, over-specialized kitchen gadgets. But in truth, the best tools for the job are high-quality, multipurpose utensils. Whenever possible, choose stainless steel bowls, pans, and utensils—they'll stand up well to years of use. Unless you're into a particular kind of specialty cooking, these items should meet most of your needs:

For Cutting: One 10-inch chef's knife, one 8-inch carving knife, one 4-inch paring knife, one 10-inch by 18-inch plastic cutting board, and one knife sharpener.

For Food Preparation: One can opener, one food thermometer, one 2-cup glass measuring cup, one 4-cup glass measuring cup, one set of measuring spoons, one 3-quart mixing bowl, one 7-quart mixing bowl, one pair of tongs, one large spoon, one large slotted spoon, one large ladle, one whisk, one rubber spatula, one plastic rolling pin, one vegetable peeler, one colander, one grater, and one funnel.

For Cooking: One 10-quart lidded pasta pot, one 3-quart lidded saucepan, one 7-quart lidded saucepan, one 12-inch sauté pan, one 6-inch omelet pan, one 5- to 7-quart lidded casserole pan, one large roasting pan with roasting rack, and one trivet.

For Serving: One large glass salad bowl with salad tongs, one large serving bowl with serving spoon, two large serving platters with serving tongs.

For the Table: For the number of guests you serve regularly: dinner plates, salad plates, dessert plates, soup bowls, wine glasses, and flatware sets.

Keep a tight rein on excess utensils. Hang on to one—two, at the most—of each item, especially if only one person at a time cooks in your kitchen.

Store similar sizes and shapes together; designate a drawer for long utensils (long-handled spoons, rolling pins, and the like), a drawer for sharp utensils, a drawer for little utensils, and so forth. If you only use a certain grouping of utensils at certain times of the year (Christmas cookie cutters during the holidays, corn-on-the-cob spears and shish-kebab skewers during the summer barbecue season, pumpkin carvers in the fall), consider placing these items in labeled containers and moving them to longer-term storage so that they're not cluttering the space needed by your everyday, year-round utensils.

Again, if you choose "pretty" utensils, you don't have to hide them. Instead, display them on a rack or shelf. If you have an interesting crock jug or pottery vase, store long utensils upright in it, and then set it beside your cooking area.

Knives

A sturdy, slotted knife block stores knives safely but takes up valuable counter space. A shallow kitchen drawer makes very efficient concealed knife-storage. Line the bottom of your knife drawer with a rubberized material to keep them from sliding. Keep your knives sharp—a dull knife causes more accidents than a sharp one. If your knives are high quality and kept in good condition, the need for multiple special-purpose knives is also reduced.

Tableware

Set up shelves or a corner china cabinet to display your nicest pieces so that you can enjoy them as décor and still have them handy for table use. Place a dowel across a shelf, or a piece of molding at the edge, to keep dishes from sliding. Generously space breakable items. While this will free up your valuable cabinet space, you'll need to remember to include this area in your regular cleaning schedule so that these dishes will not only look attractive but will be ready to use. There's nothing appetizing about pulling the nice china down from display and finding cobwebs attached to them.

a note from
the instructor

YOU CAN GET BY WITH FEWER KNIVES
IF THEY'RE THE *RIGHT* KNIVES

In good condition, these five knives will take care of most, if not all, of your cutting needs. If you have the following, you can let go of most of those weird "specialty" knives:

- Large heavy knife for chopping.
- Long serrated knife for carving and slicing.
- Slender deboning knife.
- Paring knife.
- Medium-size multipurpose knife.

Protect rare or valuable dishes—and those that are seldom used—with zippered vinyl covers and foam padding. Many container stores sell boxes with dividers to keep glasses and cups from rubbing against one another. Move tableware that doesn't get used much to a less-accessible location to free up easy-access space for the items you use every day.

Flatware

Shallow drawers are perfect for storing flatware, especially if you put some kind of fabric or rubberized liner in them to keep the flatware from skittering all over the place. If your flatware drawers don't have built-in dividers to keep your items sorted by type, you can buy drawer organizers practically anywhere.

Line drawers and compartments with felt to protect nice flatware. If your collection is silver, you can buy a special type of felt that retards tarnishing.

Space flatware generously to avoid scratches. Group like items together.

KITCHEN CABINETS

Organize your cabinets according to your "micro" plans. Place spices, oils, and sauces in cabinets near food preparation areas; store re-sealable bags, paper sacks, and snack containers in cabinets near the place where you prepare school lunches. Designate the cabinet above the coffee maker for coffee, filters, creamer, and other coffee paraphernalia. Put food items and wine in cabinets away from the stove and dishwasher so that the heat from cooking and dishwashing won't affect them.

 a note from
the instructor

PLANNING A NEW KITCHEN?

If you're in the process of remodeling your kitchen or building a new house, you can choose the most efficient design from the start if you've defined your own needs clearly. Plan your new kitchen according to your own habits and patterns. Plan "micro" areas for each activity. When planning your cabinets, keep these rules of thumb in mind:

- The most efficient cabinets come in a variety of shapes and sizes rather than all one size.
- Cabinets can be designed to stretch all the way to the ceiling, providing high storage space for seldom-used items.
- Glass-fronted cabinets keep your attractive cookware safely stowed and still allow it to be on display (and you'll have less dusting to do than with open shelving).
- The interiors of cabinets can be modified for specific uses: install vertical slats and pegs for storing flat bakeware; screw hooks to the undersides to hang cups above saucers; place a turntable or pullout drawer in a cabinet for spices, etc.

Full extension drawers will increase your usuable storage space because they enable you to easily see and access items placed in the back.

A tall cabinet can be used to store brooms, mops, and a small kitchen ladder. A ladder is especially useful in the kitchen for accessing that hard–to–reach cabinet over the fridge. A high shelf in this cabinet is an ideal place to store your cleaning supplies—it keeps them away from the food and out of reach of your children.

Enhance your cabinet space with turntables to make better use of hard-to-reach cabinet areas and racks. Put shallow hooks on the inside of cabinet doors to hang lightweight flat items.

COUNTERTOPS

Keep countertops as clear and open as you can. Think of them primarily as *preparation* areas rather than storage areas. Organize your countertops so that everything on them can be removed and stored when you need extra space.

Designate countertop zones for specific activities: chopping, mixing, coffee and tea making, toast preparation, lunch packing, and so forth. Place a pullout trashcan directly under your pullout cutting board—this will save you time when you're cutting and peeling.

 a note from
the instructor

GIVE YOUR KIDS THEIR OWN KITCHEN SPACES

Giving kids the chance to prepare their own meals fosters their sense of independence, and cooking with your children is a wonderful way to create fun family memories. As you're designing your kitchen's "micro" spaces, consider including a few areas just for them.

Designate a low, easy-to-reach cabinet for their special cups, plates, and bowls, and let them choose these themselves at mealtime. Then have your children help with cleanup after dinner. Let them wash and dry their plates and stow them. This gives them hands-on experience in caring for and keeping orderly the things in their environment.

If they're old enough to help with lunch preparation (even four-year-olds can butter bread and stuff crackers into snack bags), create an area that accommodates them. Provide a stool to help them reach counter height, give them functional utensils that fit their small hands, and designate a special drawer for kid-size utensils to live in.

Remember that organization means arranging the household to serve its members—that should include its pint-sized members, too.

REFRIGERATORS

Designate specific areas in your refrigerator for each type of food. Keep uncooked meat wrapped on the lowest shelf to avoid contamination. Store cheese and butter in airtight containers so they don't pick up odors and so that they resist spoiling. Set aside a specific area for leftovers, place a piece of tape with the date on your containers, and remember to check that area when you prepare your menus. This will not only save you money but will make your meals more interesting. While you may not have the time or inclination to prepare steamed vegetables to include in your salad, those few pieces of leftover broccoli will give it a welcome twist.

Place salad veggies in airtight containers and store them in the coldest part of the fridge. Clear plastic produce drawers are ideal for storing fruits and vegetables. Take most other veggies out of their plastic produce bags so that you can see them clearly and assess their freshness.

Stay on top of the time any given food has been in the refrigerator. Label food containers with the date of purchase. Stick removable labels with the preparation date on containers of leftovers.

Schedule a specific time each week to clear aging food out of the fridge. A perfect time to do this is right before your weekly shopping trip.

a note from
the instructor

DOS AND DON'TS OF WINE STORAGE

Do store a few bottles of wine that are going to be opened and consumed within a few days. These wines will make a pleasant display if placed in a small decorative rack where you can admire their color and their attractive labels (just don't place your wine rack in the sun or near any source of heat). Before a party, bring a selection of wines out of long-term storage and place them on the rack for your guests to choose.

Do store your longer-term wine reserves in a cool, dark, quiet, relatively odor-free place. 56 to 62 degrees Fahrenheit is ideal.

Don't store unopened wine upright for long periods of time (unless it has a screw cap or synthetic cork) because natural corks dry out over time. A dry cork allows the wine to oxidize too quickly and spoil.

Don't store opened wine in the fridge—prolonged exposure (several hours or more) to cold degrades its delicate flavors.

UNCLUTTERING LESSON-END QUESTIONS

Lesson #8:

1. List each activity that takes place in your kitchen (dishwashing, lunch making, baking, etc.).

_____

_____

_____

2. For each activity you listed above, identify an area of your kitchen that you can designate for that activity.

_____

_____

_____

3. For each area, jot down ideas for ways to organize the required items.

_____

_____

_____

_____

_____

_____

clutter-free living areas

Entryways • Stairways and Halls • Dining Areas •
Gathering Rooms • Wall Hangings

ENTRIES AND FOYERS

Many of us have two separate entries into our homes: a formal front door for greeting guests, and the backdoor or the door leading in from the garage, which is frequently off the kitchen and used as the main entry for household members and close friends.

Think of the door your family uses most often as the staging area for your day. Gather what you need for each day and place it near the door so that it's ready to go. If your household uses a backdoor, you're in luck: You have a little more flexibility in the way you organize your staging area. It doesn't have to look as formal (though it must still be tidy), and the objects you keep there don't have to vanish when company's coming.

Your staging area needs to be organized enough that the right items end up with the right household member. If time is tight in the mornings, set your staging area the night before. This eliminates the last-minute scramble, one of the greatest time-wasters and stress-makers in the average person's day.

Plan this area well, use your organizing system for it faithfully, and you might be the only person in your neighborhood who has time for a leisurely cup of coffee in the morning. Imagine yourself calmly greeting your day, full of confidence, while the families in all the other houses on your block are going through the frenzied gyrations of hunting for lost keys and sorting mismatched mittens.

As you "micro" plan this area, design a staging space for each family member. Think of the items they carry with them regularly: keys, phone, briefcase, laptop, book bag, lunchbox, purse, and so forth.

Make sure these areas are accessible to the "vertically challenged" members of your household. Don't give children shelves and hooks they can't reach.

The items your household needs will vary somewhat with the changing of seasons: sunglasses and visors give way to raincoats and windbreakers, which in turn yield to winter coats and gloves. Design your space to accommodate these phases, and place seasonal items in a storage container once the season has ended.

Whenever possible, arrange the space so that each person's staging area lines up vertically. The type of organizing you use depends on what works best for you. Some options include locker-like cubbies, or an arrangement of hooks, pegs, and shelves with a bench below for larger parcels. If you have an artistic streak, you might even create attractive nameplates for each family member's staging area. If you frequently have houseguests, leave one or two cubbies, hooks, or shelf spaces free for their items.

You'll need to design this space with a certain amount of flexibility to accommodate additional objects, like the model volcano your son built for the science fair, or the four dozen boxes of cookies you sold to coworkers during the school fundraiser. Consider hinged shelving that can be popped into place to hold volcanoes and other occasional additions to the daily load. When it's not needed, your hinged shelf can fold flush against the wall. The beauty of this—besides the extra space it creates when it's not in use—is that an empty shelf won't be standing there begging to be loaded up with clutter.

If you train yourself and your family members to place keys and bags in their staging area the moment they walk in the door, you'll eliminate the need to search for these items. Anything that won't be needed until the next morning should go immediately into its place. Items that will be in use before they go out again should be parked where they'll be needed next. Take book bags to the study area, laptops and briefcases to the home office (or whatever area you use when you work at home). Older kids can rinse lunch containers and place them beside the lunch preparation area. When you finish using an item that's going out tomorrow, place it in the staging area.

Plan your entry area to capture muddy, sandy, or wet articles of clothing before they make their way deeper into your home. If you don't have the luxury of a mudroom, designate a hanging space outside where these items can be hosed down and left to drip dry (turn wet boots and shoes upside-down), or set a plastic laundry basket nearby to catch the soiled clothing.

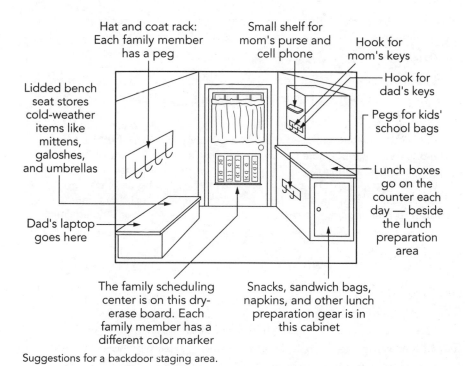

Hat and coat rack: Each family member has a peg

Small shelf for mom's purse and cell phone

Hook for mom's keys

Hook for dad's keys

Lidded bench seat stores cold-weather items like mittens, galoshes, and umbrellas

Pegs for kids' school bags

Dad's laptop goes here

Lunch boxes go on the counter each day — beside the lunch preparation area

The family scheduling center is on this dry-erase board. Each family member has a different color marker

Snacks, sandwich bags, napkins, and other lunch preparation gear is in this cabinet

Suggestions for a backdoor staging area.

What about nonroutine items you bring home, like parcels from shopping? The only way to keep them from cluttering up your staging area, or languishing in any other part of the house, is to make a plan for the items before you buy them. Schedule enough time at the end of your shopping trip to allow for putting the new purchases away. Decide what you're getting before you shop, and designate a space for each new item. As soon as you bring parcels home, unwrap them and place them in the spaces you've created for them.

If your home has only one entrance, the door must serve dual purposes: staging area and welcoming area. If your entry or foyer has a large coat closet, consider setting up your staging area inside it so that you can close it when you have visitors. If you don't have a closet, consider concealing most of the stuff in a bench with a hinged seat lid, and add a lightweight cabinet unit above it. Key hooks can screw into the inside of a cabinet—or even into the door of the cabinet—just as easily as they screw into a wall.

 a note from
the instructor

THE ART OF KEY MANAGEMENT

You're sure you had them in your pants pocket last night, but now they've vanished. Maybe you dropped them when you went back out to the car. As you dig madly through sofa cushions and dirty laundry, you're praying frantically that your toddler didn't flush them down the toilet again.

Wouldn't you love to take back all those frazzled moments that you spent searching for your keys? I can offer you the next best thing: four steps to organizing your keys so that they'll never waste your time again:

1. Designate a single spot to keep all keys and key rings: a rack of hooks, key cabinet, or drawer of small containers.

2. Label or color-code each hook or container to identify which key goes there.

3. Label or color-code each key (or set of keys) to coordinate with its designated hook or container. Use plastic key tags or the colored plastic loops that go around the head of the key.

4. Place keys back in their designated spaces after every use.

HALLWAYS AND STAIRS

In general, hallways and stairs should not be used for storage. It's against the law to store anything on a stairway because it creates an emergency evacuation hazard (but *under* the stairway is a prime candidate for ingenious storage). Hallways should be kept as clear as possible, but you can probably get away with a few shallow shelves, pegs, and hooks. Let's look at a few of the ways you can squeeze at least a few storage solutions into these tricky areas.

Dark, stuffy, cluttered hallways are a perfect way to ruin the ambience of a home. If you're storing any large items or boxes in your hallway, begin by clearing everything out and giving the hall a good cleaning. Then attend to the lighting. Even a long, windowless hallway is less oppressive when it's clear and well lit.

Next, decide which of your storage needs is best suited to the limited type of storage a hallway can provide. It's the perfect place to display framed photos and artwork, tapestries, and relatively flat collections (dishes, textiles, or collections in shallow display cases). If your hallway is wide enough, you might be able to mount a few shallow bookshelves, or knock out a section of wall and install recessed shelving and cabinetry (unless you have a blueprint of your home's structural members and know what you're doing, hire a contractor). A long, shallow hall table may provide a few drawers for small items.

In general, think of seldom-used display items or collections for hallway storage. If you're spending a lot of time standing in the middle of the hallway fishing around for your possessions, you risk becoming a sort of clutter yourself. Also, hallways are typically high-visibility, first-impression areas, so tidiness and aesthetics are essential.

The number one consideration with staircases is safety. Some people place statues or potted plants on wide staircases, but even this can be dangerous. We assume that a staircase is for stepping on; we're not expecting to negotiate around objects on stairs, so we're unlikely to be on the lookout for them, particularly when we're coming down the stairs half-asleep in the morning or the middle of the night. But the walls around your staircase can probably safely accommodate a few pictures and flat display items. If you have a broad enough landing, you might also sneak in some shallow bookshelves or even a shallow curio.

Under the staircase is another story. This is a terrific place for storage—it's hardly suitable for anything else. Custom cabinets and shelves with that unique "under-stairs" shape can add a quirky charm to your décor. Since the under-stairs area probably shares space with your living room, this is an ideal place to store craft items that you work on while watching TV or chatting with company.

DINING ROOMS

The dining room is a perfect place to practice the hide-it-or-display-it rule. A dining room overloaded with stacks of china and crowded with wall hangings can create enough visual noise to cause indigestion. Your "macro" plan for this room (assuming that you're actually using it for dining) should focus mostly on out-of-sight storage, and a few aesthetic display pieces. Keep it attractive but simple.

Sideboards provide ideal freestanding storage for dining areas because they offer both spacious cabinets for unsightly items and shelving for display pieces. They also feature a long serving surface for buffet items or for staging tableware before it goes onto the table.

Many people install built-in, floor-to-ceiling cabinets in their dining area to make room for an array of dining accessories without creating a cluttered appearance. If your dining room doesn't have such cabinets and can't accommodate them, a shallow armoire or china cabinet (particularly one that fits into a corner) can offer similar benefits.

 a note from
the instructor

TABLECLOTH STORAGE

It's tricky to store fine tablecloths in table-ready condition. In general, the fewer folds you put in fine fabrics, the better they'll hold up. Consider deep shelves and drawers where your tablecloths can lie folded in quarters. You can also hang towel racks inside your dining room cabinets (possibly even on the insides of the cabinet doors) and drape your tablecloths over them for wrinkle-free storage.

A single high shelf above the dining area, running the length of the room, can create a terrific spot to display your nicest pieces of tableware—particularly heirlooms and antiques that are too nice, or too fragile, to actually serve food on. Consider recessed or track lighting to make these areas a focal point.

LIVING ROOMS AND GREAT ROOMS

What's the "macro" plan for your main living area? Is it a formal entertaining space for guests or a place where the family can kick back and watch a movie without worrying too much about spilling popcorn on the rug? Is it a room for everyone to gather to enjoy their favorite hobbies (will one person sew while another sculpts) or the primary focal point of a single activity (music, reading, or watching sports)? The typical living room is a multipurpose room shared by everyone in the household.

a note from
the instructor

THE BENEFITS OF HIDING YOUR TV

I like the idea of an entertainment center that closes when it's not in use because it tastefully conceals the TV. Television and movies certainly have their place in our lives, but we overuse them and, in doing so, miss out on a lot of wonderful opportunities to simply sit and talk. Which do you think is more likely to deepen your relationship with your family and friends: an hour of conversation or an hour of spacing out in front of the tube?

I understand why we do it. It's so easy to flip on the TV and slide into neutral. Meaningful conversation takes effort.

That's why I like the thought of a TV stowed away behind cabinet doors; you have to make a conscious decision to watch it. It's not as much of a reflex. It allows you to stop for a moment and consider other activities.

This is especially important if you have children and you're concerned about the amount of TV they watch. Setting up your living room so that the TV isn't the room's automatic focal point is a great way to reinforce your values.

There are additional benefits you can gain by hiding your TV. A room with an attractive painting or piece of furniture as a focal point is more pleasing than one that features a TV. According to the practice of feng shui, a blank TV screen is considered negative energy—it steals life from the room (for more information on feng shui, see *The Learning Annex Presents Feng Shui*).

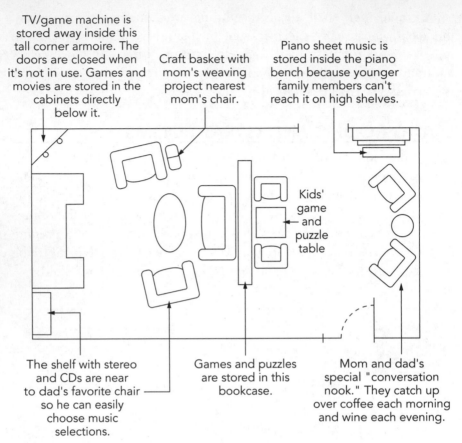

TV/game machine is stored away inside this tall corner armoire. The doors are closed when it's not in use. Games and movies are stored in the cabinets directly below it.

Craft basket with mom's weaving project nearest mom's chair.

Piano sheet music is stored inside the piano bench because younger family members can't reach it on high shelves.

Kids' game and puzzle table

The shelf with stereo and CDs are near to dad's favorite chair so he can easily choose music selections.

Games and puzzles are stored in this bookcase.

Mom and dad's special "conversation nook." They catch up over coffee each morning and wine each evening.

Example of macro-planning in one family's living room.

As you're creating your organizational plan for the living room, start by defining its functions. Identify all the activities that will take place there. Think of each member of your household—what special activities will they do in this room?

Next, make a sketch of the room. Experiment with pencil drawings until you've mapped out a workable area for each activity. Now consider the storage requirements for these activities.

If your living area must host a wide variety of activities, consider dividing it into "sub-rooms."

Designate a quiet conversation corner, a movie-watching area, a games, crafts, and activities area, and so forth. Make partitions for the different areas of your living room out of storage pieces such as bookcases, trunks, freestanding cabinets, and armoires; arrange your furniture and rugs to accommodate these different activities.

WALL DISPLAYS

Bare walls make a house feel austere, but poorly planned wall décor can make a room look cluttered and chaotic. Make sure your wall displays are an asset to the room by planning them in advance.

Group photos and artwork in similar frames (ones that are either identical or have complimentary colors and textures). To arrange a wall, cut out paper the same shape as all the frames you want to hang. Experiment by taping up the paper until you like the arrangement. Then hang the real thing.

When displaying collections on shelves, place like items together. Consider grouping large items in pairs or in threes.

Nothing draws the eye to display items like focused lighting. Track lights and recessed lights that swivel will give your display an almost museum-like importance and add a tremendous elegance to the room. Consider recessed lighting for display shelves and cabinets.

UNCLUTTERING LESSON-END QUESTIONS

Lesson #9:

1. Sketch or describe the area surrounding the door your family uses the most.

_____

_____

_____

_____

2. Assign a portion of this area to each family member.

_____

_____

_____

_____

_____

3. For each family member, list the items he or she needs to take along to school or work each day.

_____

_____

_____

_____

_____

4. Jot down or sketch any ideas you have for organizing each person's area to accommodate his or her items; for instance, pegs for book bags and coats, shelves for books and purses, and hooks for keys.

_____

_____

_____

_____

_____

5. Sketch or describe your living room.

_____

_____

_____

_____

_____

6. List all the activities that take place in your living room.

_____

_____

_____

_____

_____

7. Assign an area of your living room for each activity.

_____

_____

_____

_____

_____

8. Jot down or sketch any ideas you have for organizing each activity space.

_____

_____

_____

_____

_____

clutter-free bedrooms

Master Bedrooms • Children's Rooms • Bedroom Closets •
Dressers • Nightstands

We get into trouble when it comes to keeping our bedrooms organized. They're private, they're usually at the back of the house, and they have a door, so it sometimes seems easier to pile all manner of stuff from every other room in the house into our bedrooms and slam the door when company's coming.

The problem comes when we try to retire after a stressful day and can't seem to unwind. The bedroom is causing just as much anxiety and frustration as the outside world because it's chaotic and disorderly.

We also use our bedrooms as multipurpose rooms. They often double as workout rooms, home offices, hobby studios, and laundry-folding centers. When we try to unwind and fall asleep at night, we're surrounded by unfinished chores and reminders of work.

In today's super-stressed world, it's more important than ever for your bedroom to be a calming retreat; it should be a place waiting to ease you conveniently into sleep at the end of the day. I recommend that you reserve your bedroom solely for resting and sleeping. Whenever you enter the bedroom, you'll send your mind and body the signal that it's time to let go and relax. In fact, some psychologists recommend that you use your bed only for sleeping—even reading and TV-watching should take place elsewhere—and that you should climb into bed only when you're ready to sleep. While this strategy might be helpful for many, I've also known some people who can't fall asleep unless they read themselves to sleep snuggled under the covers.

Unfortunately, many of us don't have the luxury of using our bedrooms only for sleeping. City-dwellers are often so pressed for space that every room must serve multiple functions.

If your bedroom has to pull double-duty, at least try to isolate these activities from the sleeping and relaxing spaces. When you "macro" plan your bedroom, look for ways to delineate these areas. Place your desk in an alcove and draw a curtain across it when it's not in use, or set it up in a closet or armoire so that it can vanish behind a door when the day's work is done. Best of all, put the whole thing on a wheeled cart so that your entire office can roll away to another part of the house when you need to clear out the "noise" of unfinished business.

Hide your exercise equipment behind a screen or curtain, or invest in the models that fold away into a closet. Dumbbells and mats can be stowed in attractive chests, baskets, or boxes.

If you fold laundry in your bedroom, consider using a collapsible table that can rest in a closet when not in use. Hide the iron, starch, and mending items out of sight at the end of your laundry session as well.

Once you've managed to delegate nonrelaxing activities to other rooms—or, if they must stay in the bedroom, tucked them out of sight—you can focus on accommodating the activities that help you relax. Do you enjoy knitting, reading, writing, or listening to music in bed? Set up your bedroom to make these activities as stress-free as possible. Keep a knitting basket parked beside your bed with all the items you'll need for your nightly knitting session. Set your books, reading light, and reading glasses on your bedside table, and consider a bolster, a set of firm pillows, or a padded headboard to prop you comfortably while you read. Whatever you prefer to do to unwind at the end of the day, organize the space near your bed so that the activity is ready and waiting for you.

I'm tempted to discourage people from watching TV in bed. I think it adds more to our stress rather than reducing it. I realize, though, that many people aren't willing to give it up, so if you must have a TV in your bedroom, you'll probably get better-quality sleep if you can hide it away when it's not in use. Consider stowing it in an armoire or small entertainment cabinet so that you can close the doors and make the TV vanish when it's time to sleep.

MASTER BEDROOMS

Organizing the master bedroom is less of a challenge if you're single. If it's a haven for the two of you, it has to accommodate two unique—and sometimes extremely different—sets of habits.

When you share a bedroom, it's a given that you *won't* have exactly the same needs—or the same level of neatness. I'll go into greater detail on coping with a disorganized spouse in Lesson 14, but until we get there, let's focus on setting up the room for both your bedroom activities and your mate's.

Micro-Planning for Two

Do you like to read in bed late at night, even though your spouse has to get up early? Or does your mate work the night shift and resent the fact that you're up and into the lotus position by 4:00 a.m.? Although your different bedroom habits may seem incompatible now, you'll be amazed at how many diverse preferences can be accommodated with a little bit of careful organization and "micro" planning.

Make the decision at the outset to respect both partners' bedroom habits, and commit to finding ways to honor them. Read with a book light, watch TV with a set of headphones, hang an opaque curtain between the bed and your yoga area.

Storage Solutions in the Master Bedroom

By now I hope that as you look at a large piece of furniture in your home, you're not just admiring its aesthetic allure but also visualizing its potential storage capacity. The jumbo-sized bed that the master bedroom can accommodate is also a jumbo-sized *storage opportunity*.

a note from
the instructor

MAKING ROOM FOR THE TWO OF YOU

It's a sore subject with nearly every couple, to one degree or another. It often starts long before the quarrels about money or the battles over raising the kids, and it can persist long after money ceases to be tight and the kids have moved away. Every couple must work through the inconveniences and annoyances that arise whenever two adults live in a shared space.

"I have to wrestle my way through a jungle of drip-drying pantyhose to reach the shower," he complains.

"He's got these horrible gingham sheets with *ducks* all over them," she groans.

How can two unique individuals live peacefully in the same environment? They compromise. They learn to tolerate each other's diverse tastes and behaviors wherever they can, and they talk out a mutually respectful solution to the rest.

When I work with couples who are struggling to inhabit the same home, I encourage them to list their goals. Focusing on the things that are mutually beneficial takes away some of the urge to blame each other. It's more constructive to start from, "We'd like a space where we can cozy up and read together" than to point the finger by saying "That tie-dyed bedspread of yours gives me migraines!"

From there it's a matter of talking it out, learning what's important to the other, and deciding together how best to reach those shared goals. When you've worked together to create an environment that serves your relationships, even soggy pantyhose and gingham ducks become easier to tolerate.

For starters, think in terms of boxes and drawers on casters that can fit under the bed. Put your bed on lifts to increase your storage space, but don't stop there. Some beds today come with headboards that feature built-in storage. A cedar blanket chest or steamer trunk at the foot of the bed is a fine place for extra blankets and comforters.

If you have room, an armoire is a wonderful addition to your bedroom. Not only can it be an attractive piece of furniture, it's a versatile storage unit. If you have limited closet space, you can outfit it to provide added hanging storage, or you can have it lined with shelves for storing folded garments, your yoga mat, or linens for your bed.

Use the architectural features of your bedroom: alcoves, recesses, and niches. Consider a high shelf running along the tops of the walls.

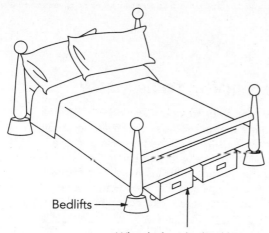

Bedlifts

Wheeled under-bed boxes

Bed lifts enable you to store larger boxes and drawers beneath your bed.

Any unused space is potential storage space. There's one caveat here: Refrain from hanging heavy artwork or shelves directly over the bed. It can be physically dangerous and can disturb your sleep if you worry subconsciously about things falling on you during the night.

CHILDREN'S ROOMS

Children's rooms need to be simultaneously a great place to sleep, to play, and to study. As you "macro"-plan, create clearly defined spaces in your child's room for each of these activities.

Most parents can't put the words "kids" and "organization" into the same sentence without smirking. Many of my students complain that their children flatly refuse to join their organizing campaigns. If this issue becomes too much of a battleground at some point, you'll simply have to let it go. However, you'll probably meet with a lot less resistance if you start when your kids are young and involve them in the planning.

My students often plead, "Will *you* talk to my kids and sell them on how important it is for them to get with this program?" When I do talk to the kids, I invariably get a sense that they feel as though something's being imposed on them.

"But my mom won't let me pick out the stuff I like," complained one teenage girl. "She insists on this horrible white wicker furniture for my room, and I *hate* it!"

a note from
the instructor

GIVE THEM *SOME* ROOM TO BE MESSY

Don't get too obsessive about having your kids put away one toy before taking out another. A friend told me that her toddler kept insisting on playing with wooden trains and Lincoln Logs at the same time. He put up a fuss whenever Mom told him to pick up one before opening the bin with the other. She finally discovered the reason for his insistence: He wanted to build his own trains out of the Lincoln Logs and then run them on the wooden track. In combining the two toys, he was expressing his creativity!

When I asked her what kind of furniture she'd have if she had the choice, she answered that she wanted a few modern, hip pieces that she could rearrange as her needs and interests changed. I asked her if she'd be willing to organize her own activities if she had the furniture that would meet her needs. She answered enthusiastically.

The mom capitulated. Today, her daughter's room is still not exactly the paragon of neatness, but it at least has the look and feel of "contained chaos."

Involve your kids in the process from the beginning. Talk to them about their interests and needs. This can be a real eye-opener; it may reveal interests you didn't realize they had. Then discuss ways you could set up their rooms to serve those interests. Encourage them to brainstorm with you, and respect their wishes.

In many cases they know better than you do what will work for them. Design the room to accommodate their needs and their size. Have you ever visited a Montessori classroom? It's called a "children's house" for good reason—everything's tiny. Chairs, tables, shelves, even sinks and toilets are low enough for them to reach with ease. Students feel that it's truly *their* classroom because it's designed for their needs.

You can organize your children's rooms with this principle in mind. Choose desks and chairs to fit them, place shelving at their hand height, and make sure that their possessions are accessible.

I recommend flexible furniture for children's rooms because their needs are always changing. You can now find a wide selection of furniture designed to grow with your kids: cribs that become toddler beds, changing tables that turn into dressers, and a wide array of adjustable desks and shelving that can be raised to accommodate a growing child.

Store toys as you would other items: some stowed and some on display. Make sure that every toy has a designated space, and be patient with your kids as they learn where everything goes. Try not to have too many toys on display at once—don't overwhelm them with choices. Just try to keep toys accessible and easy to clean up.

Don't become obsessive about the mess—a certain amount of chaos is inevitable. Just make sure that when it's time to clean up, they can manage it. Parents often scold, "Clean up this mess!" at children too young to really understand what "cleaning up" means. No one is born knowing how to organize. You have to teach them how to do it. Simplify the process for them, and do it with them until they get the hang of it.

A child's room is a great place to put storage containers to unconventional uses. A hanging shoe bag with multiple pockets makes a great stuffed toy keeper. Many stores sell versatile wooden cubes that you can paint to match the child's room. These can be stacked in any combination to provide toy storage. For numerous small toys (toy cars, action figures, small plastic animals) consider a rack or shelf that will accommodate a row of clear plastic containers or lightweight mesh baskets.

Plan a few areas that allow them to express their creativity. Keep some shelf space clear to showcase artwork and other projects. Make some room on one wall to display paintings and drawings. Cover it with cork and fabric so that the child can pin up artwork, or hang a few easy-access picture frames and then change what's on display every few months. Let your kids choose what they'd like to put in the frames.

Keep in mind that you're not just organizing a room, you're fostering a lifetime of organizing habits. You probably won't succeed if you simply impose order upon your kids. If you involve them in the decisions, in a friendly, supportive way, you'll be happier with the results.

BEDROOM CLOSETS

In an ideal world, even your dressing area would be separate from the room where you relax and sleep. If you happen to have a small, unused room adjacent to your bedroom, consider turning it into a dressing room. Line the walls with rods and shelves and place a bench in the middle. Create a dedicated area for laundry where you can stow your dirty clothes until you wash them or take them to the drycleaner. Today's hampers are more attractive and versatile than ever, often providing multiple bins to allow you to separate lights, darks, and delicate items. If you don't have a separate room to devote to your wardrobe, at least try to reserve your bedroom closets for your clothing and personal items. When you open the closet to grab a sweatshirt, you shouldn't have to wrestle your way past the vacuum cleaner.

Bedroom closets need to be organized enough to create a sense of calm order. If you get stressed out every time you go looking for a particular scarf or tie, your closet isn't serving you well.

This should be one of the first places to tackle on your organizing list. Somehow, tidy closets create a domino effect. Getting your closets shipshape generates a certain momentum that will help you get the rest of the house under control.

The more that's adjustable in a bedroom closet, the better—especially rods. Hang delicate items, clothing that must keep its shape (like blazers), and clothes made from silk, velvet, and other impressionable fabrics. Leave a little space between hanging items if you can. Hang long items together, and use the space under short ones for bins. Mount hooks on the inside of the door for ties, scarves, and other accessories.

You probably dress in the same spot each morning, but I'll bet you've never really thought of it as a "dressing area." You'll find your morning routine a lot easier if you consciously create a spot for dressing. Light it well, hang a full-length mirror nearby, and create a place for staging the day's wardrobe selections. If you're pressed for time in the mornings, lay out the day's clothes the night before.

If you have room, you may want to consider placing a vanity adjacent to this area. It's an ideal place to complete your morning routine and provides a perfect storage area for your cosmetics and hair care products.

DRESSERS

Choose dressers with drawers that aren't too deep. It's difficult to use the space wisely in deep drawers. Customize each drawer to serve a specific purpose. Keep your drawers from becoming a tangled mess by placing dividers or smaller containers inside them. Decide what type of organizers you need first, though, or the organizers themselves will become clutter and will turn everything inside them into clutter.

If you do end up with a few deep drawers, use them to hold heavy sweaters, T-shirts, jeans, exercise clothes, and home clothes. You might also find them handy for extra blankets and comforters.

Keep jewelry and small accessories in shallow drawers, or stack several shallow containers. Plastic egg crates and ice cube trays work great for earrings and brooches. Slide your delicate necklaces inside plastic drinking straws so they won't get tangled and broken.

NIGHTSTANDS

Consider your needs before you purchase a nightstand. If you already have a serviceable dresser, you may not need an enormous nightstand with additional drawers. If you only need space for a book, an alarm clock, and a glass of water, a modest side table will do the trick. If it has open space beneath it, you could slide in a single decorative box or basket. For small bedrooms that won't accommodate a table or nightstand, mount a shelf beside the bed to serve the same purpose. For *very* small bedrooms, choose a headboard with a built-in shelf area (*behind*, rather than *above* your head, where the fear of falling objects might disturb your sleep), and consider wall-mounted lighting.

UNCLUTTERING LESSON-END QUESTIONS

Lesson #10:

1. What activities do you enjoy doing in bed at the end of the day?

_____

_____

_____

2. What changes could you make to your bedroom to make these activities easier and more enjoyable?

_____

_____

_____

3. List any aspects of your bedroom over which you and your mate disagree (décor, furniture arrangement, etc.).

_____

_____

_____

4. Jot down ideas for ways to satisfy both your wishes and your mate's, or list ways you might compromise.

_____

_____

_____

5. Ask your kids for their opinions on ways to organize their rooms. Write them in the space below. Revisit what you've written in a week or two from now. Objectively, which of your kids' ideas are doable? How many can you commit to doing?

_____

_____

_____

Other Thoughts:

_____

_____

_____

_____

_____

_____

clutter-free bathrooms

Toiletries • Medications • Towels

The bathroom is yet another repository for a never-ending array of gizmos. Hair curlers, beard trimmers, toiletries, and cosmetics of every description—they all pile into the extremely limited space most bathrooms provide, and they take up permanent residence whether they're ever used again or not. One of my students habitually brought back travel-size shampoos from every hotel she visited. She traveled a *lot*. When I gathered up all the little bottles and counted them, they totaled 218. We whittled the collection down to 100, and from there, we got her down to 40. We put them in an ornate basket and set them out for her guests to use.

Start by clearing your bathroom of excess junk. Pick the razor that you like best and discard the rest. Weed out the cosmetics you never use. Give your excess toiletries (in nearly new condition only) to a senior center; they'll make delightful gifts during the holidays.

Keep your bathroom functional by storing only what you need there. Don't lug home a 12-pack of hair mousse from your local warehouse store and expect to fit the entire package under the sink. If you do buy in bulk, keep only what you use over a short period of time in the bathroom and store the rest elsewhere. Refill a small, attractive container of hand soap from a larger container in the hall closet. When you buy in bulk you also need to be mindful of a product's shelf life. What seems like a bargain at the time may not be because many creams and cosmetics have a limited shelf life.

"Macro" planning the bathroom is not as straightforward as it may seem. A lot of activities must take place in a very small space, so the more you can do to utilize that space well, the more efficient your bathroom will be. If your bathroom is tiny (how many times have you heard someone complain that their bathroom is too big?), you can still put the space that you have to better use. Most of the area around your toilet goes to waste. Organizers call this "dead space." There's not a lot of it, but there's enough that it could store at least *something*—how about a couple of spare rolls of paper? A little reading material?

Even in the tiniest cubicle there's usually room for a narrow shelf or two. A more costly option is recessed shelving. If necessary, you can even install small glass shelves across the window. If your bathroom feels really cramped, consider adding more mirrors—they make any room seem bigger.

 a note from the instructor

BATHROOM SAFETY HAZARDS

I can't count the number of times I've visited a friend's bathroom and discovered an electrocution waiting to happen. I've seen radio cords draped directly across bathtubs, electric curling irons sitting in a puddle of soapy water on the counter, and plugged in hair dryers poised where they could plop into the toilet. Many people take unnecessary risks with electrical appliances in the bathroom.

Avoid a deadly accident by minimizing the number of electrical items you use in your bathroom. Never leave curling irons, hot curlers, or similar devices plugged in unattended. Never pass an electrical cord over an open toilet bowl, tub, or sink. Consider buying a hair dryer that mounts on the wall so that you'll avoid the temptation to prop it where it might fall into the sink. Unplug all electrical devices and store them after use.

a note from
the instructor

8 WAYS TO MAKE A TINY BATHROOM FEEL BIGGER

1. Install more mirrors.
2. Install a shelving/cabinet unit above the toilet.
3. Install recessed shelving.
4. Mount shelving or pullout drawers in the cabinet under the sink.
5. Mount high shelving near the ceiling.
6. Hang storage pockets from the back of the bathroom door.
7. In the shower, use hanging shower caddies, shower curtains with pockets, and wire baskets that mount on the wall with suction cups.
8. Hang a rack from the ceiling, or an extra tension rod in the shower, for towels and laundry.

Besides lack of space, the other major concern with bathrooms is keeping them as clean and dry as possible. Keep a bucket or plastic tote filled with bathroom cleaning supplies so that they're readily accessible. Be careful what you store in bathrooms; the heat, humidity, and germs can wreak havoc with fabrics, papers, medications, and cosmetics. Store only what's necessary, and keep your bathroom as clean and airy as you can.

TOILETRIES

It's important to containerize toiletries because many of them are numerous and tiny, like cotton swabs and manicure implements. Store razors in a jar or glass, cotton swabs in a tall upright container, and all nail trimming gear in an appropriate-sized container. Fill small, pretty bottles with the lotions, soaps, and other items that you use frequently; store the larger containers in a closet.

Organize the space under the sink to hold toiletries. Be sure that you store them in waterproof containers to safeguard them in the event of a leak under your sink. Don't jam so many items in the space under the sink that you won't notice a leak (or be able to reach the shutoff valve) if one occurs. If you still can't find room for all your toiletries, use the back of the bathroom door—this is the perfect space to hang a set of wall pockets made from linen or plastic.

a note from
the instructor

SHOULD WE CALL THEM TOILETRIES CABINETS?

I don't know why we call them medicine cabinets; they're terrible places to store medicines. They're not bad for toiletries though. Think of your medicine cabinet as a mini-closet. Give it the same micro-planning attention you'd give your other closets. Devote specific areas of your cabinet to grooming, cosmetics, and so forth. Do a periodic "sweep" of the contents to discard clutter, and then return each serviceable item to its designated place.

Sort through your toiletries a few times a year and discard the ones you no longer use. Check your makeup items periodically—some makeup products can spoil or dry up over time. If you have a lot of a certain makeup color or product that you've fallen out of love with, why not donate it to a women's shelter if the makeup is still in good condition?

If you use a lot of makeup, consider devoting an entire cabinet or rolling basket cart to organizing it. Store like items together: Designate a container for mascara, another for blush, another for lipstick, and so forth. If you apply your makeup in the bathroom, make sure you have ample lighting and countertop space to do the job efficiently. Consider mounting a retractable mirror with a swing arm in your makeup prep area. That mirror can serve double duty because it's also useful for shaving.

If you're one of the lucky few who has a large bathroom, this is another good place for a vanity. It provides a perfect means to separate your cosmetics from other bathroom paraphernalia, and it ensures that you have everything you need within arm's reach.

MEDICATIONS

Don't store medicines in the bathroom—heat and humidity alter their effectiveness. Try a linen closet or kitchen shelf instead. Stay on top of the expiration dates of medications, and throw them away when they expire. Even sunscreen loses its effectiveness over time. Also dispose of leftover medications unless your doctor specifies otherwise.

Keep first aid kits ready with everything you might need in the event of an emergency. Keep one in the kitchen (where most cuts and burns happen) and another in a central location (the linen closet is often close to the center of the house); make sure they are within easy reach of everyone except small children. Store all your first aid supplies together, and examine them from time to time to make sure they're still in usable condition.

 a note from
the instructor

THE FAMILY FIRST AID KIT

The American Academy of Pediatrics recommends that you keep these basic first aid supplies on hand at all times. They'll prepare you for most household emergencies. Keep only one of each!

- Acetaminophen for pain relief (or aspirin, with your doctor's approval).
- Antihistamine for allergies and bee stings.
- Syrup of ipecac to induce vomiting (replace this every year).
- Triangular bandage for wrapping an injury or making a sling.
- Elastic wraps for sprains.
- Disposable instant-activating ice bags.
- Various sizes of adhesive bandages, including butterfly bandages.
- Adhesive tape.
- Scissors with rounded tips.
- Safety pins.
- Tweezers.
- Mild antibacterial soap.
- Petroleum jelly.
- Antibacterial ointment.
- Rubbing alcohol.
- Cotton swabs or balls.
- Thermometers—both oral and rectal.
- Roll of gauze, plus 2-inch and 4-inch gauze pads for dressing wounds.
- A first-aid chart or easy first-aid book to guide you in handling injuries.

TOWELS

Towels are one of those items that you always want to have within reach when you really need them. I believe it's necessary to have at least a small amount of towel storage in the bathroom itself, even if your linen closet is close by.

Even in the tiniest of bathrooms, there's probably room for a high shelf large enough to accommodate a stack or two of extra towels. If you have the room, mount a towel cabinet—these look especially nice with glass doors. If you're crafty, you might choose to pick up a small glass-fronted curio cabinet or display case at an antique store, refinish it in a nice clean bathroom color, and use it in the bathroom as a towel locker.

Plan ahead for those inevitable occasions when you have more damp towels than racks to hang them. Keep a folding drip-dry rack, small decorative ladder, or similar device handy.

Give each of your houseguests a set of towels in a distinguishable color. Keep dark towels for makeup removal, and wash them separately.

If you don't have a designated destination for dirty towels, they'll end up all over the place. Avoid throwing them into the hamper with clothing—you don't want a mildewed towel cohabitating with your nicest blouse until wash day.

Don't leave it up to chance. If you have the space available, stow a removable laundry hamper somewhere in the bathroom. If you can't keep it in the bathroom itself, try to stash it as near as possible (wherever towels are most likely to end up after family members discard them).

 a note from
the instructor

DON'T SKIMP ON TOWEL QUALITY

Some items can end up costing you more if you're too thrifty. Don't skimp on towel quality, for instance—it's simply not worth it. I advise my students to buy higher-quality towels. They last longer, keep their colors better, won't fray as easily, and their fluffier texture feels nice on a chilly morning.

a note from
the instructor

ADD A LITTLE STYLE TO YOUR BATHROOM

It's a perfect combination just waiting to happen. You have a nice collection of little silver cups or small colored bottles and no place to put them; your bathroom has dozens of makeup brushes, beard combs, tweezers, and other small items, and no containers to keep them organized. With a little ingenuity you can create stylish storage in your bathroom.

Use a collection of egg cups for small makeup accessories or an assortment of small, attractive bottles to hold small quantities of soaps and lotions. If you have a favorite mirror and no place to hang it, consider having a medicine cabinet designed to fit behind it so that the mirror becomes your medicine cabinet door. With a little creativity, bathroom storage can be stylish and practical.

Do the members of your family wear their towels from the bathroom to their bedrooms? If they do, you're probably frustrated at the daily number of soggy towels you have to peel up from the carpet, the middle of the bed, out from under the dog, or wherever else they may have landed. If you can't coax your family into dressing in the bathroom (many people don't like to do this because of the steam) or wearing a bathrobe for the walk to their rooms, you may have to accommodate their behavior with a designated wet-towel area in the bedroom. A well-placed hook, peg, or small towel bar near their dressing area may do the trick.

UNCLUTTERING LESSON-END QUESTIONS

Lesson #11:

1. List all the activities you do in the bathroom (for instance, applying makeup, trimming toenails, or drying hair).

_____

_____

_____

2. How many of these activities could be moved to a different room where there's more space available?

_____

_____

_____

3. Sketch or describe your bathroom. Where are the potential storage areas?

_____

_____

_____

4. For each of the potential storage areas you've identified above, list the items you might store there.

_____

_____

_____

clutter-free offices

Office Organization • Offices at Home • Fold-Away Offices • Desks • Chairs • Computer Areas • Supplies

Regardless of the type of work you do, an enormous part of your success depends on the organization of your workspace. Whether you work at home or away, your office must facilitate your work.

Among your primary goals when you "macro" plan your office are to:

- Keep your business running efficiently.
- Automate and streamline the mundane tasks of running your business so that you can focus on the work that brings success and financial reward.
- Create an environment that inspires you.

We've spent the bulk of this book focusing on your home, but the organizing principles you've applied to your kitchen, bathroom, and dining room apply just as well to your office: Arrange your workspace to meet your individual needs, "micro" organize your work area to accommodate all your tasks, apply your creativity to storage spaces and containers, keep only what you use, and automate wherever possible.

ORGANIZING YOUR OFFICE

It's imperative that you maintain complete control over your workspace. Keep everything centrally located; all items pertaining to your work must stay together.

Your office area should facilitate your individual work habits. There's no such thing as a one-layout-suits-all office arrangement. The key to organizing your office is to know your own needs and preferences.

In general, try to arrange the tools you use regularly so that they're within arm's reach. Many people place their filing cabinets across the room from their desks, creating the need to hop up from their seats and walk across the room whenever they need a file. While that may work for files that you don't use regularly, you should place your active filing cabinet next to your desk—this will save you time by keeping the files you need regularly an arm's length away.

 a note from the instructor

DESK CONFIGURATION FOR EFFICIENT WRITING/RESEARCHING

If your job requires you to work with a lot of papers, here's a two-desk arrangement that Los Angeles-based literary manager Ken Atchity finds effective:

Desk 1: The primary workstation. Use an L-shaped desk: half for your computer and half for organizing and reference. Keep your most important reference books, inbox, and phone here, but leave most of the space open.

Desk 2: The reference and research station positioned behind or to the side of Desk 1. Keep your other reference materials and active files here, along with your printer.

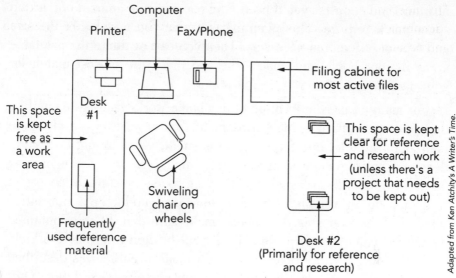

Desk arrangement for a writer or editor.

Two efficient furniture arrangements for offices are L and U shapes, especially when combined with a swiveling chair. This configuration gives you lots of desk surface to create your "micro" stations for various tasks.

Do you walk into your office each morning only to be greeted by the sight of several untidy mounds of paperwork spreading across your desk? Whatever your particular work situation, organize your paper flow so that everything stays within its own category, whether you organize it by subject, urgency, or chronology.

Remember that organizing paperwork is about *processing*. Assign a home to each piece of paper. Sort everything into Action, Reference, and Project files, or into your outbox if you're delegating it to someone else. Never let your papers degenerate into disorganized heaps. This will sap your productivity like nothing else.

HOME OFFICES

When you decide to create an office area at home, start with the "macro" plan. Outline your activities and inventory your needs. List the furniture and supplies you'll need, and consider the amount of desktop space you'll require. This planning will give you an idea of the size and type of office area necessary. Then you can evaluate the available areas in your home and choose the one that's the closest match for your needs.

For many of us, the location of our home workspace is dictated by the constraints of our living environment. You may have a single spare bedroom available, but if your home is small, you may not be able to devote an entire room to your work. You might have to resort to carving out a tiny niche. In extremely small living spaces, you might choose to fit a cupboard or armoire with a fold-down desk and keep a mini-office inside it. Whatever area you choose, make sure that it's self-contained so that you can close it up and make it vanish when you finish working. You can do this with a door (either to a room or cabinet as described above), a screen, or even by hanging an attractive piece of fabric. Otherwise, you run the risk of being unable to mentally separate your personal life from your work life.

When you're deciding where to locate your home office, evaluate how well you can work in a given location. How much distraction can you tolerate? Some people need absolute quiet when they work, while others prefer a certain amount of background commotion.

How much natural light do you need? Do you need to get up and pace when you work? Should you be near the kitchen so that you can quickly grab a snack without breaking your work rhythm, or would easy-access snacks, combined with work tension, prove disastrous to both your waistline and your bottom line? Whatever your particular work needs, choose (or create) the space that supports them best.

When you plan your home office, be sure to consider the tax implications. If you plan to claim a tax deduction for the part of your home that serves as your home office, be sure to store only business-related items there. Even if you have excess storage available, you should not store any nonbusiness items there (such as clothes, games, or toys). In determining your tax status and potential deductions, be sure to check with your accountant or financial advisor.

TEMPORARY OFFICES

As mentioned above, even if your workspace shares the same four walls as your living space, I think it's a good idea to keep your professional life separate from your home life by at least a visual barrier. For many of us the mere sight of our workspace, with its nagging unfinished business and threatening deadlines, creates stress. If you can never "get away" from the office, how will you recharge for the next workday?

a note from
the instructor

CONVENTION CLUTTER-BUSTERS

My students frequently complain about the massive amounts of junk they end up dragging home from conventions. It's incredible how many freebies get pressed into our hands when we're busy meeting and greeting: pens, binders, letter openers, key chains, and mini flashlights. One friend discovered a convention booth giving away potted bonsai plants. Try bringing one of those on an airplane!

At the time, it often seems easier to stuff all these items into our briefcases and tote them home to sort later. Then, of course, we get busy with something else and haphazardly toss those ill-considered promotional gimmies into our desk drawers. Keep in mind that the companies that give away these freebies aren't doing so to help you restock your office. These items aren't really office supplies; they're *advertising opportunities*.

You don't need to turn your workspace into a cluttered billboard for other people's companies. Instead of accepting their freebies, ask for a business card. Then when the next person tries to ply you with promotional items, say something like, "Oh, thanks, but I've already got your card—let me make sure I wrote down your direct line."

Jot the date and any other pertinent contact information on the back of the card. When you get home, sort all the cards you collected into your contacts file.

If you absolutely *must* accept proffered convention freebies (if you'd risk offending your contact by refusing them), collect them all in a plastic bag or shopping tote (you'll probably get at least one of these at every convention), and then donate them to your favorite charity.

It's easiest to maintain this separation if your office is in a room or other clearly delineated area so that you can close a door or draw a curtain to signify that your work session has come to an end. If you don't have the luxury of devoting an entire area of your home to an office, or if your need for a home office is so infrequent that it doesn't make sense to occupy that much space permanently, consider creating a temporary office.

A well-planned temporary office accommodates your work habits and meets your needs while you're working, and then when it's no longer needed, it folds up and tucks away to leave that space free for other uses.

Set up an efficient temporary office of folding tables and chairs, foldout charts, and collapsing file racks. Organize everything you need in easy-access bins that can be stored with the other components of your office so that the whole thing moves as a unit. If possible, arrange your temporary workspace on a wheeled cart so that it's both self-contained and portable.

DESKS

As with all other aspects of your workspace, choose the desk that meets your individual needs. Ideally, your desk should be both highly functional and aesthetically pleasing—both will positively affect your productivity.

If your desk is an antique or has a fragile surface, cover the top of your desk with glass, linen, canvas, or leather to protect it.

Where should you position your desk? Wherever it's most conducive to your work. If you like to look out the window while you work, position it with a view out the window. If you'll frequently greet visitors in your office, you'll probably be more comfortable with a direct view to the door. However, if you're in the "visual stream" where you make frequent eye contact with people outside of your office, then you'll have more interruptions. Recognize your needs and work habits, and arrange your space to accommodate them.

CHAIRS

A student of mine once proudly showed me his gorgeous new home office. It was beautifully appointed, and the centerpiece of it all was his brand new modern-style office chair. When I complimented him on the beauty of the chair, he replied, "Yeah, it looks good, but it kills my back. I can't sit in it for more than an hour!"

Another student complained that her chair was throwing her back out of alignment, but when I recommended that she get an ergonomic chair, she said, "I can't afford one of those things!" When she later relented and bought one, she called to report that her back felt much better: "It wasn't cheap, but it cost less than what I was paying my chiropractor each month!"

It doesn't matter how impressive the rest of your office is. If your chair is torturing you, you won't work effectively.

You spend so much of your time in your chair. You owe it to yourself to eliminate as much stress as you can—especially when you consider that over time, the extra strain a bad chair inflicts on your body can add up to serious health problems.

It's possible to find a chair that's both aesthetically pleasing and ergonomic. A good chair is worth its cost. If your budget is limited, you're better off buying a high-quality used chair than a poor-quality new one.

COMPUTER STATIONS

These days our computers look as if they're staging a coup on our desktop. They're taking over, gobbling more and more of our precious workspace with a never-ending series of peripherals, wires, and extensions. You may have to resort to some creative planning to keep your computer from hogging too much of your desk space. Fortunately, many computer supply companies now make ingenious space-saving devices to help us rein in our machines.

If you set your monitor on a riser, you can scoot it back into that otherwise useless corner on your desk and use the space beneath the monitor for storage. You can even purchase a pullout keyboard shelf that conveniently stows your keyboard beneath the monitor when it's not in use. See your local computer store for other devices that may help you consolidate the space that computers, keyboards, CPUs, and peripherals eat up. Consider a space-saving flat-screen monitor; they've dropped in price considerably over the last few years. Many of these monitors now come with built-in speakers, which eliminate two more pieces of hardware on your desktop.

Don't let your computer's cables and wires commandeer your workspace, either. Mount your power strip to the underside of the desk. Some computer stores sell special baskets designed to hold your computer cables; these baskets mount to the underside of your desk. Be sure to label each cable and wire. Consider using some of the plastic tubing that's available for corralling bundles of cable. For phone cords, try a retractable cord-keeper that will wind up excess cord at the touch of a button. These are especially good for temporary offices.

A student of mine mentioned recently that she uses bread ties to organize her jungle of cables. This can be dangerous, since bread ties have metal wires imbedded in them and can be an electrical hazard. Hardware and computer stores sell special plastic ties that are designed to bundle cords of all types, so use them instead.

COMPUTER FILES

In today's automated world we have not one but two desktops. While the clutter that accumulates on your computer isn't physical, the mess that it causes is as distracting and disruptive as the clutter on your "traditional" desktop. If we don't keep our files organized, we can waste just as much time hunting for lost computer files as we can for three-dimensional objects.

It's important to develop a system to organize your computer files; this will eliminate a cluttered computer desktop and guard against the loss of important documents. Avoid keeping several types of documents loose on your desktop. Keep your files in folders according to their type. If your files go through a sequence, create a folder for each step of the process. For instance, a writer friend keeps a folder for each step of the writing process: first draft, second draft, editorial notes, and so forth. As each manuscript passes from one stage to the next, she moves the master copy from one folder to another.

Similarly, if you run a small business, you can keep financial information this way: one folder for open invoices, another for submitted invoices, and a third for paid invoices.

Save yourself time over the long run by keeping a boilerplate file for frequently used documents. For instance, keep a formatted business letter blank with your address, a salutation, and a closing with your name and title. Keep a boilerplate for invoices, reports, and any other documents that you use frequently.

Schedule a regular time to clean up and reorganize your computer desktop. Once a month should suffice, unless you work with *lots* of files. You could also perform this task at the end of each major project, if the work you do lends itself to this kind of organization.

Treat your computer files the same way you would paper documents— if you're unlikely to need them again, and can replace them fairly easily even if you do, throw them out. If you feel the need to keep a file for reference but you know you're not likely to need it on a regular basis, store it on a backup disk instead of cluttering your hard drive. Periodically review your floppies to weed out obsolete files.

SUPPLIES

Organize your office supplies so that you can retrieve what you need quickly and with minimum frustration. Group the items you use frequently into three categories: 1) needed several times a day (pens, blank paper, stapler, and highlighter), 2) needed every few days (blank computer disks and new file folders), and 3) needed infrequently (three ring binders and file tabs).

Place the items you need frequently close to the hand you use the most so that retrieving them takes less than a second, and returning them to their designated space is nearly effortless. Arrange the items you use every few days so that they're within arm's reach. Store the items you use infrequently within arm's reach only if there's room to do so and their presence doesn't interfere with your ability to reach higher-priority objects.

Since it's important that you leave most of your workspace free to accommodate your work, don't overload your immediate space with more items than you need. Store the bulk of forms, letterhead, and other supplies in a closet, cabinet, or armoire, and keep a small stash of these items near you in an accordion file for immediate use.

 a note from
the instructor

NEVER GET CAUGHT WITHOUT THE SUPPLIES YOU NEED

How many times have you reached for the next envelope, blank computer disk, or file folder in the supply box only to find the container empty? Running out of the supplies you need causes unnecessary frustration and disrupts your productivity.

Set up your office so that you automatically restock the items you need when your supply drops below a certain level. Keep an active shopping list close at hand so that you can add items to it as soon as you see that your supplies are running low. Schedule regular resupply trips (if you're well-organized, you'll nearly eliminate the need for last-minute dashes to the office supply store). You can also order by phone or Website—many office supply stores now waive delivery fees.

Build in automatic systems to signal when it's time to put a particular supply on the list. Drop a bright-colored half sheet of paper into your envelope box about a third of the way in. When you use the last envelope in front of the paper, put envelopes on your shopping list. Place a full sheet of bright paper on top of your last ream of computer paper. Use a bright-colored index card to do the same with computer disks and other small supplies.

a note from
the instructor

THE VANISHING PEN SYNDROME

A student at one of my seminars once reported finding a great solution to the Vanishing Pen Syndrome. His wife and kids were always raiding his workspace for pens. He would reach for a writing implement, only to find his pen cup empty.

He solved the problem by stationing family pen holders in every part of his house where pens might be needed: in the kitchen, by the phone, in his kids' rooms, and near the spot in the dining room where they liked to draw. He stocked the family's pen holders with pens that had a very different physical appearance from those he preferred to use in his office. So any of his stray pens were obviously "daddy's pens," and the others were clearly household pens. When a pen wandered outside its designated area, it was obvious.

He also moved his pen cup to a spot on his desk where he could still reach it easily, but it was out of the rest of the family's line of sight at the same time.

UNLCUTTERING LESSON-END QUESTIONS

Lesson #12:

1. Sketch or describe the layout of your office.

_____

_____

_____

_____

_____

_____

_____

_____

_____

_____

2. List all the tasks you perform in your office.

_____

_____

_____

_____

_____

3. Designate an area for each of these activities.

_____

_____

_____

_____

_____

4. Jot down all ideas you have for ways to organize these areas.

_____

_____

_____

_____

_____

5. Which areas of your office cause you the most stress?

_____

_____

_____

_____

6. List any ways you can think of to reduce the stress these areas cause you.

_____

_____

_____

_____

_____

Other Thoughts:

_____

_____

_____

_____

_____

clutter-free storage areas

Linen Closets • Laundry Rooms • Garages • Basements and Attics • Sheds

In previous lessons we've covered all the primary rooms in your home, the places where you do most of your living and working. Now let's examine the secondary areas of your home designed for storage rather than living. These areas deserve special consideration because they're the ones where clutter is most likely to stagnate.

Attics, basements, garages, sheds, and laundry areas tend to be major dumping grounds for clutter. I've had students who are literally afraid to enter these rooms in their home. They have no idea what might confront them. They have trouble even thinking of scheduling the time it will take to clear them out because they know they may be looking at entire weekends. They don't want to spend their hard-won vacation time cleaning out the garage or sweltering away in a stuffy attic.

If you've let your storage areas become mass chaos, don't despair—help is on the way. I can't promise to take all the work out of clearing out these areas, but I can offer suggestions to help you get through the task faster and with less frustration. Best of all, once you've streamlined all the items you've been holding on to, and you've created systems in each of your storage areas to containerize the items you're keeping, you'll need to spend only a minimal amount of time once or twice a year to maintain the new order you've created.

LINEN CLOSETS

My students' linen closets are often so stuffed with sheets, blankets, towels, and tablecloths that they have to tug on an item to wrench it loose. Often the entire contents of the shelf come toppling down, and everything is rounded up and jammed back in.

Frequently, they give up looking for a particular sheet set; they make do with whatever they can pry loose from the pile. If they do happen to spy a corner of the sheet set they were looking for, when they wrestled it out of the closet, they often find that it has become musty from being balled up on the back of the shelf so long. If extra supplies of toiletries are also hidden among bunched-up sheets, they may also get pelted with a rain of cotton swabs or deodorant soaps as they're tugging at that wrinkled, mildewed, or mismatched sheet.

There's a better way to store your linens.

"Micro" plan your linen closet so that like items stay together. Designate sheet shelves, towel shelves, tablecloth shelves (if you're not keeping these in your dining room storage), and extra toiletries shelves. Further subdivide your linen closet shelves, if necessary, with shelf dividers. These are especially handy for keeping tall stacks of towels from toppling. Label each shelf and subdivision. If you don't have enough room for both your linens and towels, I recommend that you find another home for your towels—preferably the bathroom.

Fold pillowcases and fitted sheets into their matching flat sheets so that you won't have to hunt for missing parts of the set. If you have several different sizes of bed sheets, designate a shelf area for each size: twin, full, queen, and king. If you have trouble telling what size a sheet is as you're putting them away, mark their sizes on an inconspicuous inside corner with a permanent fabric marker.

Comforters, quilts, blankets, bedspreads, and mattress pads are so voluminous that they take up more than their fair share of closet space if they're folded like other bed linens. Try storing them in specially designed space-saving bags to keep them compact and protected. Another option for storing bulky blankets or comforters is a cedar chest.

Keep your towels sorted by frequency of use; store everyday bath towels separate from hand towels and guest towels. Store guest towels together on a high shelf so the kids don't use them to dry the dog.

If you store tablecloths in your linen closet, try to hang rather than fold them. If there's room, mount dowels on the inside of the linen closet door and drape tablecloths there, or hang tablecloths on hangers. Remember that the fewer folds you put in them, the nicer they'll look on the table.

Resist the temptation to overstuff linen closet shelves. The first time you have to resort to yanking, you could undo all your hard-won organizing. If your storage space is extremely limited, then in addition to storing your towels in another area, you may want to store sheets in a flat container under the bed for which they're intended. Rotate the position of the items in your linen closet regularly so that they don't get musty; place freshly laundered towels and sheets on the bottom of the stack so that everything gets used evenly.

LAUNDRY ROOMS

Unless you hire out your laundering, odds are you'll need more than just a place to stash your washer and dryer. You'll also need a clean, well-organized place to *process* your laundry.

Some of the "micro" tasks in the laundry room include sorting (pre-wash and post-wash), stain scrubbing, mending, pre-soaking, hand washing, air-drying, folding, hanging, and ironing. On top of that, you'll need convenient areas to store laundry supplies.

Consider installing shelves above the washer and dryer for soaps, softeners, and stain removers, plus mending kits, mesh garment bags, hangers, irons, and a basket or bin of clothespins if you have a drip-dry line.

If the space above the washer and dryer is not conducive to hanging shelves, consider buying freestanding units on casters. These are specifically designed for the laundry area. Also invest in folding drying racks; these can either slip into the space between the washer and dryer or hang flush against a wall until needed.

If at all possible, try to create a clean, sturdy flat surface for scrubbing stains and mending small tears. A collapsible ironing board can pull double duty in this capacity, or you might choose to install a shelf that folds down when it's not in use. If you'll also use this shelf for folding, make sure it's fairly large. Cover the shelf with flannel or canvas to protect your garments.

Stow several collapsible drying racks in your laundry area. You'll end up using them for much more than drying freshly washed items. They'll also come in handy for hanging bathroom rugs, throw rugs, floor mats, and the like when these items are awaiting washing, and they're a convenient place to hang wet items (to prevent mildew) that you won't be able to wash until later.

If space is tight, sort your laundry into color-coded canvas or mesh bags instead of baskets. These bags can hang on the wall out of the way until the clothes are ready for the machine. To save the time it takes to rematch pairs of socks after washing, some of my students pin pairs of socks together with safety pins. Others use the shorthand method—they buy only one style of white socks and one style of black socks.

Cut down on handwashing by placing your delicate items in mesh bags and washing them in the machine on a gentle cycle. If your machine is small and you must wash large items like comforters, consider visiting a laundromat (their larger machines will do a better job of washing big, bulky items) or having the items professionally laundered. It's frustrating to tie up your machine for a long cycle only to discover an unrinsed blot of laundry soap in the middle of your comforter.

If your basement is the ideal spot for your laundry area, make sure that it's dry. If it's not, consider using a dehumidifier. It doesn't do any good to clean your laundry and then let it hang in a damp basement.

After drying, sort clean clothes by category and intended destination: bedrooms, linen closet, and so forth.

GARAGES

If your garage is so cluttered that you can't fit a bicycle inside, much less a car, you're wasting a valuable portion of your home. Unless you live in an extremely temperate climate, your car will be better off inside the protection of your garage. It will last longer, and it will cost you less to maintain its appearance. A garage is also a perfect spot for large, bulky, or dirty items that would be impractical to store inside your home.

If you can manage to squeeze a car inside but little else, your garage is probably the first area of your home you see each day as you return from work. If it's cluttered and depressing—a constant, shameful reminder of your untidiness and neglect—this daily downer may affect your mood.

Especially if cleaning your garage is likely to be an all-day (or multiple-day) mission, get your entire family involved. Plan and discuss your cleaning strategy the day before. Give each person a specific task. Consider coordinating your garage-clearing with a garage sale the following weekend. After your garage is clean and reorganized, you should only need to devote an hour or two each spring and fall to keeping it in good order.

Start by removing everything from the garage and sorting it into categories. Once everything is sorted into categories, inventory what you have, and get rid of any items that you no longer use, are duplicates, or no longer function properly. While your garage is empty, I strongly recommend that you take the opportunity to give it a good cleaning before anything goes back in.

Now that your garage is clean and cleared of clutter, redefine its spaces and assign a home to every item that will be stored in your garage. Garages are ideal places to make use of the vertical storage space available on walls because they don't have to meet the same aesthetic standards as "living" areas of the house.

Most hardware stores sell heavy-duty hooks for large items like bicycles (in addition to freeing-up valuable floor space, you will extend the life of your tires by hanging your bicycle), strollers, skis, and ladders. It will save you enormous amounts of floor space to get these items up and out of the way. Likewise with large, cumbersome tools such as rakes and clippers. These will store nicely on a section of pegboard. Here's a trick I learned from my grandfather: Draw the outline of each tool on the pegboard or wall so you can quickly return it to its proper place.

If your garage has open rafters, don't forget to use them. They can be terrific places to store long, flat items. Stash summer window screens there in winter, and then swap them out for storm windows in the summer. If your roof is tall enough, you can lay plywood across the rafters and make a small crawlspace for storing nearly anything.

Shelf storage may also come in handy in your garage. You can find a variety of shelving units in large hardware stores, or you can build shelves to conform to your space. Items that are well-suited to shelf storage include gardening products, car-care products, and small hardware items. Be sure to dedicate an area for each type of storage, label it, and use appropriate containers to house the various items.

Plastic bins of all sorts work well for gardening supplies. Consider using small, covered trash containers to store soil and soil additives. A caddy with a handle works well to store and tote hand-held gardening tools, while tightly sealed containers work well for pesticides. Be sure to label these clearly and keep them on a high shelf out of the reach of children and pets.

Car-care products are also well suited to plastic storage. Wax, polish, a polishing cloth, and touch-up paint will fit nicely into a covered box. You can use a bucket to efficiently store sponges and drying rags for washing your car.

Out of necessity, hardware stores have become a prime example of effective organization. With thousands of small items to organize, they would be in complete disarray without well-designed bins and containers. One of my favorite types of organizing products creates a similar type of storage at home. It's a hard plastic or metal box with small, compartmentalized drawers that separate the various types and sizes of nails, washers, nuts, and bolts. Hardware stores carry these in a variety of sizes to accommodate different storage needs.

 a note from
the instructor

GARAGE SALE TIPS

- Advertise your garage sale in the local free classified papers.
- Make sure your signs are clear and readable from the road.
- Arm yourself with change the night before: ones, fives, and coins.
- Brace yourself for a barrage of "early birds," or specify "no early birds" in your advertising.
- Price your items to move.
- Take the remainders to a charity after the sale.

While garages make ideal storage areas for a wide variety of items, there are certain things that you should never store there. The smell of gasoline, oil, and exhaust can permeate clothing, fabrics, and upholstered furniture, rendering them unusable. You also run the risk of damaging stored papers or photos if your garage tends to be damp.

BASEMENTS AND ATTICS

Basements and attics are often the biggest stumbling blocks on the road to an organized lifestyle. Many of my students have exhibited a great deal of anxiety at the very idea of clearing out and organizing their attics or basements. These areas can be emotionally charged—they often contain memorabilia and keepsakes that their owners, or other family members, have accumulated or inherited over the years.

My students have taught me that the process of letting go gets easier with time and practice, so you may want to save these emotion-piquing areas in your home for the end.

Basements and attics are classic clutter catchers. It's all too easy to keep shoving seldom-used items into them until they become unnavigable. We always think we'll have more time later to deal with the boxes, bags, and bins that we're unable to sort through now, but we never *have* the time unless we *schedule* the time.

If we let this go on long enough—after years or even decades of accumulation—we may have to find enough time to go through *hundreds* of musty boxes.

 a note from
the instructor

FIVE THINGS *NOT* TO STORE IN YOUR ATTIC OR BASEMENT

1. Foods (unless canned).
2. Electronics.
3. Photos.
4. Vital documents.
5. Flammable or corrosive chemicals.

Basement and attic storage is also problematic in another way. Students often lament that they stored their precious keepsakes in their basement or attic only to discover—when they retrieved those items years later—that their irreplaceable treasures had been ruined by dampness or extreme changes in temperature.

If your attic and basement are stuffed, tackle them the same way you did the garage: Make it a family event. Turn attic cleaning into a treasure hunt. Encourage each family member to gather up keepsakes they find in the attic that are particularly meaningful to them, and take responsibility for cleaning and repacking them at the end of the task.

Once you've gotten your attic or basement under control, and you're ready to rethink their usage, remember that these areas are long-term storage for durable stuff only. Don't store food in these areas unless it's canned or in a freezer; don't store fabrics unless they're placed in airtight containers; don't store photos, electronics, tapes, or discs.

Roll up rugs and cover them in plastic or butcher paper. Label and wrap framed items with foam around their corners and thin foam or felt over the glass to protect it.

Draw or tape a "no clutter" line in your basement around boilers, oil tanks, furnaces, etc., and keep them clear.

Finished basements are becoming increasingly popular. Maybe you're even more desperate for extra living space than you are for extra storage. In that case, consider finishing off an unfinished basement and converting it to a hobby room, recreation room, den, or library. Just make sure you resolve any dampness problems before you begin your refinishing project.

Attics may also be refinished as living spaces as long as there's adequate ventilation, heating, and cooling. An attic loft makes a terrific studio or office, particularly for someone who needs to work without distractions. Finished attics also make cool bedrooms for teenagers.

SHEDS

Sheds have become increasingly popular in suburban and rural areas. Many of the sheds available today are attractive enough that they can be placed in full view of your home, making them both functional and an asset to the aesthetics your yard.

The advantage of sheds is that they give you all the benefits of off-site storage without being truly off site. They're also a terrific place to store dirty items (like lawnmowers, plumbing snakes, and garden tools) and chemicals that are too hazardous to store inside the house.

Think of your shed as a garage in miniature; use the vertical spaces on the walls, tuck items into recessed areas, and make use of rafter areas.

Some municipalities and homeowner's associations have rules preventing or limiting the installation or construction of sheds. Be sure to check local regulations in advance to avoid the expense and effort of installing something that will need to be removed.

UNCLUTTERING LESSON-END QUESTIONS

Lesson #13:

1. List all the items in your linen closet that are not linens, blankets, towels, or bathroom supplies.

   _____

   _____

   _____

2. For each of the items above, list at least one alternative storage space. Consider moving it there.

   _____

   _____

   _____

3. Are you avoiding cleaning out your garage, basement, or attic for emotional reasons (for instance, fear of confronting the past, hoarding possessions, or shame)? If so, describe those emotions here.

   _____

   _____

   _____

4. Write out a plan for dejunking your garage. List the steps involved. Assign a date and time. Give each family member a job. Decide how you'll celebrate when the task is complete.

_____

_____

_____

5. Do the same for your attic.

_____

_____

_____

6. Do the same for your basement.

_____

_____

_____

Other Thoughts:

_____

_____

_____

_____

_____

_____

lesson 14

clutter-free families

Enlisting the Family's Cooperation • Raising Organized Kids • How to Live with a Disorganized Spouse

If you live alone, the task of maintaining your organizing systems is fairly straightforward. But what if you have other household members to factor into the equation? What if you've got a spouse or kids who aren't exactly crazy about your new zeal to revolutionize their environment?

"My kids are always undoing my organizing," one student complained. "For every step I take forward, they drag me two steps back."

"My husband absolutely refuses to work with me on the daily 10 minute pickup," explained another. "And he's responsible for 90% of the mess!"

It's sometimes difficult to enlist the cooperation of the rest of the household, even though the rewards of organization will ultimately benefit them, too. Let's examine a few of the ways you can help your family embrace their new organized lifestyle—or at least make it easier for *you* to embrace it.

GETTING THE FAMILY ON BOARD

When family organizing strategies fail, it's generally not because the plan isn't workable—it's because family members feel that something's being imposed upon them, and they get their backs up. Children—especially toddlers and teens—are notorious for this, but spouses aren't immune to it either. And if we look at it from their perspective, we can see why such a proposal might be unwelcome: No one likes being told what to do.

Your best bet for eliciting your family's cooperation is not to impose your system on them; instead, you should involve them in its creation from the beginning. You may first have to use a bit of psychology. Sell them on the numerous benefits of organizing before you even mention the commitment required. Give them concrete examples of the ways organization will improve their lives:

> "Wouldn't it be nice to spend that extra 10 minutes watching cartoons each morning instead of looking around for lost sneakers?"

> "With the money we save not having to replace the household items we can't find, we could buy the camcorder we've all wanted for capturing special family moments."

> "Can you imagine how cozy this room would feel if we got rid of those stacks of old newspapers and magazines? We could set up a special little nook right here just to hang out, talk, and read."

Here's another incentive—if the whole family participates in the de-cluttering process (including the basement, attic, and garage), you can sell unwanted items online, at a consignment shop, or at a garage sale and then spend the proceeds on a family vacation. Give everyone a vote on the destination. If a vacation's not feasible, divide the proceeds equally, and let everyone spend their share however they wish.

Once you have their attention and have sold them on the rewards, explain to them that you'd like to make this change as a family and that you welcome their ideas. Help each family member find ways to contribute to the de-junking process, and involve them in "macro" planning the household. Respect their ideas and their preferences. Make sure that it's always *our* project, never *my* project.

Once your family is organized, how do you make sure it stays that way? Once again, involve everybody in planning the maintenance routines that will keep the system shipshape. Call a family meeting and outline the activities that need to happen, and then discuss how to divvy them up. Let family members choose the activities they prefer whenever possible. If they bicker over a particularly "choice" assignment, suggest that they can have the good assignment if they'll also take on one that everyone finds odious. Take the time to work it out. Test drive the new routine for a couple of weeks, and then meet again to iron out the kinks.

Remember that organization is a learned behavior—it doesn't come naturally to many of us—and that family members, particularly younger ones, will require a great deal of encouragement, training, and patience. It's worth the up-front investment for the grief it will save you in the long run.

Give Everyone Personal and Household Organizing Responsibilities

It helps to divide organizing chores into two varieties: personal and household. Everyone takes personal responsibility for organizing their own clothes, possessions, and rooms; they also have a certain number of chores they do to serve the household.

For instance, a teenager's personal organizing might include making her bed each morning, rounding up her school books after dinner, and tidying up her room each evening. In addition to her personal maintenance routines, she's responsible for loading the dishwasher after dinner, straightening the living room, and helping her younger siblings lay out clothes for the next day. On the weekends, she helps sort the laundry, folds her clean laundry and puts it away, and then assists Dad with grocery shopping.

Even very young children can perform some chores. A four-year-old can empty a wastebasket, put toys and games away, and put books back into a bookcase. Small children often ask, "Can I help?" when they see other family members performing a chore. Tap into their natural desire to imitate us big folks. Let them feel that they have something important to contribute.

Make sure that both the personal and household responsibilities each family member takes on are appropriate to his or her age. Define each task as clearly as possible, and provide whatever job training is needed.

Coordinate Chores

Do the best you can to foster a spirit of fun and cooperation where household tasks are concerned. Give everyone the option of rotating tasks so that no single chore becomes too much of a burden. If anybody complains that they hate a particular chore, give them the option of swapping with someone who doesn't mind it as much. For instance, if you hate clearing out the refrigerator before the weekly trip to the grocery store, but your wife doesn't mind it, offer to trade that chore for a chore that she hates.

Try to give everyone a well-rounded variety. Make sure each person has some kitchen duty, some yard work, and some general household maintenance. And be appreciative! When they finish a task early, or take the initiative to organize an area not on their list, praise their good work.

	Jack	Patti	Libby	Dad	Mom
Personal	• Pick up own toys and clothes • Make bed	• Pick up own clothes and books • Tidy room • Make bed	• Pick up own clothes and books • Tidy room • Make bed	• Put away personal items	• Put away personal items
House	• Set table at dinner	• Wash and dry dishes w/L	• Wash and dry dishes w/P • Help with cooking	• Repairs as needed • Cooking (alt. w/M)	• Cooking (alt. w/D)
Yard	• Feed and water Boris	• Cut grass (alt. w/L) • Water garden	• Cut grass (alt. w/P) • Pick up twigs	• Swimming pool maint.	• Garden maint.
Saturday	• Empty wastebaskets	• Dust and vacuum • Shop w/D (alt. w/L)	• Change linens • Shop w/D (alt. w/P)	• Grocery shopping	• Laundry

One family's chore board.

Coordinate Schedules

"I never know when anybody's going to be home for dinner," lamented one of my students, a busy mom of three. "My oldest works a rotating shift at the movie theater, my middle kid has play rehearsal until eight or nine each night, and my youngest goes to soccer practice several afternoons every week."

Take the guesswork out of family scheduling by creating a family coordination center in a major gathering area (a kitchen wall works well). Invest in a large, dry erase board to schedule everyone's activities. If you use the board to map out the week or the month, you can assign a different color dry erase pen for each family member. Schedule a regular time to update the board.

This is also an ideal place to keep personal and household chore lists. You might even choose to laminate each person's list and use a wipe-off marker to check off each item as it's completed.

RAISING CLUTTER-FREE KIDS

While it's true that organization is a learned behavior, it's not a foreign concept to most kids. Children go through phases in which they're quite attuned to organizing principles, the state of their environment, and the concept of personal ownership. If you're involved with your kids, you can capitalize on these interests and help focus these natural tendencies into sound organizing principles that will last them a lifetime.

Start Early

Good organizational habits are easiest to instill when you start from the beginning. Kids who are raised from early childhood with daily routines and a sense that everything has its place are typically more secure and better adjusted. The organizing skills they learn when they're young will serve them for a lifetime.

Timing is an important factor in teaching organizing skills. If you can catch them at a teachable moment, your efforts will be enhanced. Observe the way they play; some time between the ages of two and six, they'll go through a phase in which organizing is a natural part of their games. They'll sort all their cars by color, all their animals by species, and all their blocks by size. It only takes a little shaping from you to turn those games into organizing practice: "Let's see if we can play this color game with your T-shirts...."

Help them organize their lives in a way that supports their independence. Choose clothing for them that they can put on and take off by themselves. Until they're six or older, they'll probably struggle with tying shoelaces; circumnavigate that frustration by buying them shoes that close with Velcro. If they can make their own sandwiches, place bread, peanut butter, cheese slices, and a spreading knife on a low shelf in the fridge. Buy a mini pitcher and fill it only halfway so that it's easy for them to pour their own drinks.

Help them learn that everything has a place. Label shelves, drawers and cabinets—at least until they get the hang of where everything goes. Even children who are too young to read can learn to do this. Instead of placing word labels, draw pictures of the objects that belong in each drawer and paste them up in place of worded labels. This project by itself makes for a fun way to spend the afternoon with your child. If you're not wild about drawing, cut the pictures out of a magazine, or take a snapshot of the item and paste it on the container.

You'll get further and avoid getting their backs up if you accentuate the positive. Accommodate the activities they enjoy; work with them to create clever, efficient, and simple ways to store all the paraphernalia they need to accommodate their various interests and activities. Show them creative ways to display their collections. Encourage them to keep track of what they have, and give away, sell, or throw away anything that they are no longer using or enjoying on a regular basis. Set limits on the number of things they can possess.

Teach Them Pride in Their Environment

Visit any Montessori classroom, and you'll see kids as young as three washing tables, arranging flowers, sorting pencils, and working diligently to keep their environment tidy. How is this accomplished? These kids work so hard because they know that the classroom is *theirs*. Create this atmosphere at home by giving your kids their own spaces to care for and take pride in.

Be Clear, Patient, and Positive

Especially with younger kids, parents often fail to elicit the cooperation they had hoped for because they give their children responsibilities that aren't appropriate for their age. Make sure your children are really ready for any given task. They'll have the skill and the attention span to sort socks long before they're ready to sort *all* their laundry. Don't give them more responsibility than they can handle.

Be very clear about what each task requires. Spell it out for them, walk them through the steps, and show them what level of performance is acceptable. It's all right to leave a few faint smudges when they're cleaning a window (if they're young), but if you can still make out a whole *handprint*, the job's not done yet.

Keep it light, fun, and rewarding. Praise their efforts. Nothing will lose their cooperation faster than threats and force. Be patient, and stay positive.

Model the Behavior

None of this is going to work if you don't set an example for your child to follow. You can't hold them to a standard you're not willing to uphold yourself. Let them see what you expect of them by modeling it for them.

LIVING CLUTTER-FREE WITH A SLOPPY SPOUSE

I've seen marriages suffer severe damage due to clutter. Arguments over lost keys, unpaid bills, and scattered newspapers can strain a relationship. The more organized spouse resents having to live in chaos; the disorganized one resents being told how to live.

The following sections describe a few of the options you should explore in order to create a more peaceful environment.

Sell the Benefits

Approach your mate when he or she is calm and receptive. If necessary, ask to schedule some time to talk—this way you'll have his or her undivided attention, and he or she won't resent you for interrupting something. Plus, the act of formally scheduling time to discuss the issue will place it in a context of importance.

Explain all the benefits the two of you will enjoy by becoming more organized. Demonstrate the tangible rewards: the afternoon spent relaxing in the backyard instead of cleaning out the garage. List the financial savings on items that won't need to be replaced as often. Think of hobbies or interests your mate would like to pursue, and propose the idea that some of the newly cleared space will be available for that purpose.

Keep your discussion short, amicable, and goal-oriented. Ask your mate if he or she would like to talk about it further, and ask for ideas and suggestions.

Don't badger. If your mate's not interested, drop it for a while. If you persist, you're more likely to get a hostile response. If he or she shows an interest, try to schedule another talk to begin the planning.

At your next planning meeting, let your mate have the floor first as a show of goodwill. If he or she is on board, the project now belongs to the two of you—always treat it as a collaboration.

Provide the Environment

If you don't get anywhere with peaceful discussion, quietly begin the project on your own. Dejunk and organize a few rooms at a time—particularly those rooms in which organization will provide the most benefit to your mate. After living for a while in the clean, inviting, organized space you've created, your mate may become addicted to it.

 a note from
the instructor

HIRE SOME HELP

Couples argue frequently over the division of household labor. If you take into account the fact that millions of women now work full time, it's a wonder that any couple can perform all of the necessary family chores and have any free time remaining to enjoy each other's company. Add children to the mix and the little bit of free time that may have existed quickly disappears. When families lack adequate time to talk about their problems and feelings—and when everyone's going through each day constantly stressed out—it's no wonder that conflicts constantly arise.

It may be time to revive an old custom. In our parents' day, even modest middle-income families frequently hired a cleaning person to come in once or twice a week to help lighten the load—and that was in the days when Mom stayed home with the kids full time. If it worked for our parents, maybe it can work for us.

Consider the benefits of delegating the most frustrating and time-consuming household chores to a hired helper. You and your spouse will be free to spend more time on meaningful things: deepening your relationship and pursuing your dreams. At the very least, it will alleviate the next argument over whose turn it is to do the laundry.

If All Else Fails, Let It Be

Have you had the sloppiness argument with your mate so many times that you could write the lines down from memory? Maybe it's time to stop trying to reform him or her, and instead start searching for ingenious ways to minimize the impact.

Design around his or her habits, and try to accommodate the quirks. Does he always drop his socks in the same spot on the bedroom floor? Stick a laundry basket right there. Does she pour a cup of coffee before the pot's done brewing, leaving a sticky mess? Get a coffee pot with an automatic pause feature. Does he squeeze the toothpaste tube all wrong? Buy one for him and one for you.

If you've tried everything else, and you're at the end of your rope, it might work to divvy up the house. You could rework your "macro" plan to turn your home into a virtual duplex with his and her living spaces. Your mate can keep his/her portion his/her way; you can keep your portion your way. You're still living together, you still see each other, but you don't have to be bogged down by your spouse's disorganized habit.

It's not a terribly attractive option, and it becomes an extremely tricky proposition if you still have kids living at home. But if that's what it takes for the two of you to live in peace (and for you to have the organized environment you need), try it. At least it's better than having the same dirty sock argument for the thousandth time.

UNCLUTTERING LESSON-END QUESTIONS

Lesson #14:

1. Do you and your kids argue regularly about organizing? Do you fear that your children's resistance to organization will set them up for a lifetime of self-defeating habits? Identify your fears and frustrations and write them here.

_____

_____

_____

2. List your goals for getting your family organized; for instance, you might write, "Space available for family game night." Think about what each family member could do to help the family achieve these goals.

_____

_____

_____

3. List all regular household chores and the frequency with which they need to be done. Devise a system that allows each family member to rotate through the list of chores so that nobody gets stuck with the same chores over and over again.

_____

_____

_____

4. What rewards could you offer your kids daily, weekly, and per task for completing various organizational chores?

_____

_____

_____

5. Is your spouse disorganized? Write down all the sloppy habits he or she has that drive you crazy.

_____

_____

_____

6. For each habit you listed above, jot down any ideas you have for ways you can cope with the habit.

_____

_____

_____

7. Are there any habits of yours that drive your spouse crazy?

_____

_____

_____

8. What could you do differently to make these habits less annoying?

_____

_____

_____

Other Thoughts:

_____

_____

_____

_____

_____

_____

time management

Effective Scheduling • Making the Most of Your Time

The name of this lesson is something of a misnomer. The truth is, you *can't* manage time. As time-management consultant Harold Taylor put it, you can only manage yourself in relation to time. But the way you organize your relationship to time can make the difference between success and failure, whether you're running a household or a corporation.

Remember, we make 80 percent of our results from 20 percent of our efforts, so be very selective about how you spend your time, and evaluate what return you'll receive from performing a particular task. Does the return that you receive support your goals?

Let's look at some of the ways you can schedule your activities and cut down on interruptions so that you can make the best of the time you have.

a note from the instructor

SCHEDULING TIPS

- Figure out what's most important to you and schedule it first. This doesn't necessarily mean that your most important task has to be the first thing you do, but it should be the first thing you *schedule* when you look at your calendar and evaluate your available time and the deadlines you need to meet. Also, it's important that you be clear on what your most important task is. It may be the task that's most critical (e.g., preparing your taxes so that you can meet the April 15 filing date), or the task that you enjoy the most (e.g., scheduling time to meet that favorite cousin you haven't seen in five years and who'll be in town for only one day). It's simply a matter of planning ahead and prioritizing.
- Occasionally block out a day or a week in which you don't take any new appointments.
- When you calculate the completion time of a project, add extra time to your estimate (some people advise that you *double* your time estimate).
- If you have to cancel an appointment, reschedule it right away so you don't forget.
- Don't procrastinate.

PRINCIPLES OF EFFICIENT SCHEDULING

Many people resist scheduling their day because they believe that rigidly structuring every minute will add to their anxiety and make them feel constricted and trapped. They're thinking of it backward. It's not a question of taking 16 waking hours each day and finding ways to stuff every hour to the gills—it's a matter of taking those activities that are important enough to schedule and organizing them in the order that makes the most sense.

In effect, you're doing with your day what you've just finished doing with your rooms and closets: You're weeding out the clutter (of wasted time and meaningless activities) to clear the way for what matters most to you.

Habitually overstuffing your day will quickly lead to burnout. One of the priorities you must maintain, even on the busiest days, is unscheduled time. Sadly, in today's fast-paced world, you have to *schedule* your free time if you're going to have any.

Keep in mind that your daily schedule is there precisely to prevent you from becoming overwhelmed, not to keep you incessantly marching through your day like an overly wound-up toy. It exists to serve *you*; if you end up feeling as though you're serving *it*, it's time to re-examine your scheduling habits.

Map Your Time

Create a time map on your computer with a separate column for each day of the week and a separate row for each half-hour time increment between rising and bedtime. If you don't have access to a computer, you can create the document on a piece of paper with pen and ruler, and then make several copies so you won't have to repeat this task. First, plug in all the built-in time commitments—the ones you can't change. Then schedule the tasks and activities that offer a bit more flexibility.

Create your schedule around your own working rhythms. Schedule difficult tasks that require your best creativity and concentration when you're at your best; schedule no-brainers for times when your energy and concentration are on the wane.

If you're crystal clear and energetic in the morning, it doesn't make a lot of sense to exercise at that time because exercise adds energy. Instead, try to schedule your exercise for a point in your day when you could use that extra boost.

---

 a note from
the instructor

AVOID BURNOUT

- Take time off (a day, an hour, or 15 minutes) when you feel overwhelmed.
- Take lunch breaks.
- Take vacations.
- Leave your work at the office.
- Get regular sleep and exercise.
- Honor appointments that you make with yourself the same way you'd honor appointments made with someone else.
- Have a hobby.

Don't forget to schedule free time into your day. You must make it a priority to unwind, relax, and recharge. If you don't treat relaxation as seriously as any of your other commitments, something will come along to gobble up that time. The more you neglect your daily revitalization time, the less efficiently you'll work.

Keep a Daily Priority Checklist

Make a list of the tasks that must be completed that day, in order of priority. Write this list each evening, and then review and revise it every morning before you begin your day.

Don't put off unpleasant tasks—you'll make them harder to do. In general, work within your own natural rhythm. Some people prefer to tackle the most difficult task on their list first to get it out of the way; others do the fastest and easiest items first to build up some momentum for the more difficult tasks. Do what works best for you.

Group Your Tasks

You'll make more efficient use of your time if you group like activities together. Pay bills when you do your weekly budgeting; assess the errands you need to do, and then determine the best route to take so that you don't need to double back; open mail when you're handling correspondence; return phone calls that need your immediate attention right after you check your messages.

KEEP YOUR TIME PRODUCTIVE

Millions of us live our lives at a hectic pace. We rush frantically through each day believing that our time is not our own. We live with the nagging terror that all the activities we're juggling are on the verge of slipping from our grasp. You can alleviate much of this stress by observing the sanity saving, time-management rules described in the following sections.

Make Your Phone Serve You

You pay the phone bill, not the people who call you. Your phone should respond to you, not you to it. Don't permit costly interruptions.

a note from
the instructor

SEVEN MAGIC WORDS TO MAKE TELEMARKETERS LEAVE YOU ALONE

The next time a telemarketer threatens to commandeer your time, don't hang up. Whenever you simply hang up on a telemarketer, you give them permission to call you again and again. Instead, you can arm yourself with a simple phrase that *legally* prevents them from calling you back for the next 10 years, according to the Telephone Consumer Protection Act of 1991. The next time a telemarketer calls, state clearly, "Put me on your don't call list." They're legally obligated to comply.

To have your name removed from all junk mail, telemarketing, and e-mail solicitation lists, visit the Direct Marketing Association's Website at www.the-dma.org/consumers/index.html. Give them all versions of your name and those of other household members. Be sure to include misspellings.

Let your answering machine do its job. Keep a callback list with an estimated time allotment for each call—this automatically reduces telephone time.

If you're concerned that clients, friends, and family will be offended when they always get your answering machine instead of a live human being, schedule regular hours each day when you do answer the phone. Encourage people to call you during those times.

Sometimes it helps to wait a few hours—perhaps even a day, if you can—to return phone calls. You'll find that many of the issues your callers were phoning about have been resolved by the time you call back. Likewise with e-mails and faxes. Only you can be the judge of whether a given communication is truly urgent, but bear in mind that many that appear so aren't.

Before you return a call, list the items to discuss and gather any necessary information. Decide beforehand the approximate length of the call, and extend it only if necessary. If a lengthy call begins to overrun your next scheduled event, ask to reschedule and resume the call during your next available slot of telephone time.

a note from
the instructor

SIX WAYS TO KEEP TIME ON YOUR SIDE

1. **Double up mundane routine tasks.** Do some light filing or organizing while you're on the phone; balance your checkbook while you're in line at the post office. Turn moments of low productivity into opportunities to accomplish small, simple tasks.

2. **Delegate.** Whenever possible, focus on the work that *only you can do*, and delegate the tasks that anyone can do.

3. **Make phone calls before lunchtime and quitting time.** People are less willing to spend long stretches of time on the phone during these periods.

4. **Specify "no call-back necessary."** On phone messages, e-mails, and memos that don't require a response, state that the subject doesn't require a callback.

5. **Visit *them* instead of letting them visit you.** When someone asks to drop by, offer to drop by their office instead. It's easier to make a polite exit than to remove visitors who have overstayed their welcome.

6. **Be fully present.** If you've scheduled your time conscientiously, you have the luxury of focusing only on the present moment. You can avoid having past issues and future activities rob you of your energy and concentration.

UNCLUTTERING LESSON-END QUESTIONS

Lesson #15:

1. Make a chart with each day of the week and a space for every waking hour of the day. Copy the blank chart so that you can reuse it each week.

_____

_____

_____

2. Make a list of all the obligatory activities you must perform each day (those that happen at a fixed time and cannot be rescheduled—for instance, picking up the kids from school). Fill these in on your chart first.

_____

_____

_____

3. List all the activities that are most important to you, and the amount of time they require. Fill these in next.

_____

_____

_____

4. Finally, fill in time for meals, exercise, bathing and grooming, and relaxation.

_____

_____

_____

Other Thoughts:

_____

_____

_____

_____

_____

_____

ten guidelines for reducing clutter

Whether you are creating the macro- and micro-plans for each room of your house, sorting through all your possessions and deciding what to keep, or maintaining your new clutter-free system, remember these 10 important guidelines:

1. Get tough. Decide to decide.

2. Stop procrastinating. No more excuses.

3. If you're not using it, get rid of it.

4. Give it away—others may be more in need.

5. When something comes in, something must go out.

6. Less *is* more: more time, more money, more productivity, more energy.

7. Limit the space you designate for any particular activity and stick to the guidelines you set.

8. Don't keep items simply because they *may* be useful or valuable some day.

9. When traveling, set limits on what you buy. Invest in photos and memories instead of purchasing souvenirs.

10. Don't buy more than what you need of any item that is easily obtained.

appendix b

sources and suggested reading

Better Homes and Gardens. *301 Stylish Storage Ideas*. Des Moines: Meredith Books, 1998.

Hall, Dinah, and Barbara Weiss. *Storage*. London: Dorling Kindersley, 1998.

Kingston, Karen. *Clear Your Clutter With Feng Shui: Free Yourself from Physical, Mental, and Spiritual Clutter Forever*. New York: Broadway Books, 1999.

Morgenstern, Julie. *Organizing From The Inside Out: The Foolproof System for Organizing Your Home, Your Office, and Your Life*. New York: Henry Holt and Company, 1998.

Sapadin, Linda. *It's About Time: The 6 Styles of Procrastination and How to Overcome Them*. New York: Viking Press, 1996.

Sherman, Kathy Fitzgerald. *A Housekeeper is Cheaper Than a Divorce: Why You Can Afford to Hire Help and How to Get It*. Mountain View CA: Life Tools Press, 2000.

Stewart, Martha. *Good Things for Organizing*. New York: Clarkson Potter Publishers, 2001.

St. James, Elaine. *Simplify Your Work Life: Ways to Change the Way You Work So You Have More Time to Live*. New York: Hyperion, 2001.

Taylor, Harold. *Making Time Work For You: A Guide to Productive Time Management*. Time Management Consultants, 1998.

Winston, Stephanie. *Stephanie Winston's Best Organizing Tips: Quick, Simple Ways to Get Organized and Get On With Your Life*. New York: Simon & Schuster, 1995.

Winston, Stephanie. *The Organized Executive: New Ways to Manage Time, People, and the Electronic Office*. New York: Warner Books, 1994.

emergency home preparation checklist

Use this checklist to prepare your home for potential emergencies.

- Keep batteries and a portable radio readily accessible. Tune your radio to a local station.

- Recharge battery-operated equipment to full power, including cordless phones and cell phones.

- Keep a small amount of currency available.

- Make sure your household fire extinguisher is functional and that all family members of appropriate age know where it is and how to use it.

- Locate and become knowledgeable about shut-off procedures for your main gas valve, household fuse box, and water main.

- Practice using emergency safety equipment such as cook stoves, fireplaces, and lanterns.

- Back up your household and business computer files.

- Keep a backup copy of important addresses and phone numbers.

- Keep a written copy of all bank and credit card account numbers, insurance policies, and important family documents such as Social Security cards, passports, birth certificates, marriage certificates, and death certificates. Group them together in a transportable system.

- Create a spot in your home for holding batteries. Stock up on frequently used types.

- Locate and organize keys to all exterior doors, locks, and cabinets.

- Assemble a basic first aid kit. Keep it stocked and organized.

- Inventory all household goods. You may also wish to videotape your possessions and keep the tape in a separate, safe location.

- Create a list of all essential documents and the location of the originals. Store this list with a trusted peer or family member for easy access to pertinent information in the event of an emergency.

- Develop and discuss an action plan for emergencies. Determine how you'll reestablish contact in the event you're separated.

- Create a lock box with a handle for computer disks. If you have to exit in a hurry, you'll be able to grab your lock box and carry your disks to safety.

- It's critical in an emergency to have an accurate medical history. List all medications you or family members take and any operations you or your family members have had. You never know when this information may save a life. Keep a copy with you, give one to a neighbor or family member for safekeeping, and keep one in the car.

- Keep irreplaceable documents in a fire-and water-retardant safe or in a safe deposit box. Back up your computer systems and place the information in your safe or in a safe deposit box once a month.

- Keep an emergency kit in your car. Along with first aid supplies, include an old pair of tennis shoes, a jacket, and $20 in cash (to buy food or gas in case credit card service is disrupted).

■ When you're feeling depressed, anxious, or unsure what to do about real or perceived dangers, clean and organize your house. Organizing is great therapy. Dealing with the chaos outside your front door is easier if the chaos inside the front door is under control.

emergency supplies to keep on hand

You should keep the following list of emergency supplies in an area of your home that is easy to access.

- Three days' water supply (one gallon per day, per person).
- Food that won't perish at room temperature.
- Non-electric can opener and utility knife.
- Portable plastic dishpan and liquid soap.
- Several containers to collect extra water from potential water supplies.
- Heating device for cooking or defrosting food.
- Several boxes of matches.
- Waterless soap for cleaning your hands.
- Ice chest for perishable food.
- Sanitation supplies: toilet paper, kitchen bag, plastic bucket with lid, household chlorine bleach.
- Battery-operated AM/FM radio.

- $20 or more in cash and coins.
- Copies of all important documents.
- Pet supplies.
- Tools to turn off gas valves.
- Candles, battery operated lamps, or flashlights.
- Blankets or sleeping bags.
- Safe internal heating source: gas-powered heater or firewood for fireplace.
- Prescription medicine refills.
- Sturdy shoes or work boots.

appendix e

emergency
contact list

Use this form to record vital contact information in case of accidents or
emergencies. Keep this list with you at all times, and keep a copy in
your car and in your emergency supply kit.

Name: _____

Number: _____

Phone: _____

Mobile phone: _____

Insurance (name and policy number): _____

Family doctor: _____

Pediatrician: _____

Pediatric emergency: _____

Pharmacy: _____

Poison Control: _____

Allergies: _____

Medications: _____

Relatives: _____

_____

_____

_____

_____

_____

_____

Neighbors: _____

_____

_____

_____

_____

_____

_____

if your purse or wallet is stolen

If your purse or wallet is stolen, cancel all your credit cards immediately. Contact the three national credit-reporting organizations to have them immediately place a fraud alert on your credit file. Otherwise, the thief may apply for new credit in your name.

Also report stolen or misplaced Social Security cards to the Fraud Line at the Social Security Administration: (800) 269-0271, www.ssa.gov.

Equifax: (800) 685-1111,www.equifax.com.

Experian: (888) 397-3742, www.experian.com.

Trans Union: (800) 680-7289, www.transunion.com.

planning for business interruption

In the aftermath of September 11, businesses have begun to create plans for resuming operations in the event of a catastrophe. The following preparations will make any such transition go more smoothly:

Make backup copies of all computer records and maintain them offsite. Keep important documents like leases and insurance policies in a secure place with copies offsite.

Establish a temporary relocation plan. Choose a spot to regroup and resume operations in the event that you're forced to relocate temporarily. List the items and support you would need to keep your business going, and make a plan for securing them quickly should the need arise.

Meet with your employees to discuss an emergency plan. The plan should include how to safely evacuate the building and where first aid kits are located. Employees should also have a list of emergency contacts and know the locations of the closest police station, fire department, and hospital.

Review your current property insurance coverage. See
if it includes flood or earthquake coverage (most policies
don't). Review your policy deductibles and limits. Some policy
riders may cover business income for business interruption.
You may want to purchase a rider that covers the business
interruptions of your suppliers and customers.

Keep emergency supplies in stock. Keep a first aid kit,
flashlight with extra batteries, paper towels, waterproof plastic
bags, disposable camera, basic tool kit, bottled water, and
nonperishable food.

(From *Open for Business: A Disaster Planning Toolkit for the Small Business Owner*, published by the IBHS.)

Index

GREAT NEW BOOKS FROM

The Learning Annex Presents Feng Shui
By Meihwa Lin

Whether it's analyzing your house or apartment's energy flow, improving a particular aspect of your life, or just learning for fun, *The Learning Annex Presents Feng Shui* will give you the basic tools and knowledge you need to improve your feng shui and improve your life, all in just an evening.

ISBN 0-7645-4144-7 $14.99   216 pages

The Learning Annex Presents Uncluttering Your Space
By Ann T. Sullivan

From identifying your clutter patterns and taking stock of your home, to annihilating clutter room by room or even redesigning your space and your storage to keep clutter from coming back, *The Learning Annex Presents Uncluttering Your Space* helps you get your house and your life back in order.

ISBN 0-7645-4145-5 $14.99   216 pages

The Learning Annex Presents the Pleasure of Wine
By Ian Blackburn and Allison Levine

Navigating the local wine store, planning a dinner party, visiting wineries, or just ordering in a restaurant can all be intimidating. In one evening, *The Learning Annex Presents the Pleasure of Wine* demystifies wine and gives you the basic tools and knowledge you need to confidently navigate each discussion and situation.

ISBN 0-7645-4146-3 $14.99   240 pages